[

Studies of the New Testament and Its World

EDITED BY JOHN RICHES

The Reasons for Romans

The Reasons for Romans

by
A. J. M. WEDDERBURN

edited by
JOHN RICHES

T. & T. CLARK
59 GEORGE STREET
EDINBURGH

11-2-89

Copyright © T. & T. Clark Ltd, 1988

Typeset by Saxon Printing Ltd., Derby

Printed in Great Britain by Billing & Sons Ltd, Worcester

for

T. & T. CLARK LTD
59 George Street, Edinburgh EH2 2LQ

First printed 1988

British Library Cataloguing in Publication Data
Wedderburn, A. J. M.
    The reasons for Romans.
    1. Bible. N.T. Romans. Expositions
    I. Title II. Series
    227′ .106

    ISBN 0–567–09499–5

TO
BRIGITTE

CONTENTS

FOREWORD

Although much has been written, not only about Romans, but also specifically about the purpose of the letter, I feel, rightly or wrongly, that the last word has not yet been said or written on this topic. This short study is an attempt to contribute to that ongoing study, not to end it!

I have tried, in the interests of intelligibility, and of publication costs, to make this as far as possible a non-technical, non-esoteric work, and hope thereby that as many as possible of those interested in the subject-matter may find its ideas intelligible; at the same time I hope that some of my colleagues may find at least something of profit within its pages, even if my notes and my references to others' views have been kept to a minimum.

Finally, especial thanks are due to Professor Ernest Best for reading through the typescript of this work and for many helpful comments on it, including the privilege of a preview of a small section of his forthcoming *Paul and His Converts* (Edinburgh: T. & T. Clark, 1988), and also to Ms Gail Mackie for assistance in the preparation of the text, to John Riches for kindly accepting this volume for publication in the series 'Studies of the New Testament and Its World', and to Dr Geoffrey Green and Ms Elizabeth Nicol of T. & T. Clark for all their friendly help and encouragement in seeing the text through the press.

St Andrews   A.J.M.Wedderburn

I

THE ENIGMA OF ROMANS

Why Paul wrote Romans is still something of an enigma. There is as yet no consensus as to why Paul should write precisely this letter with these contents to this church at this moment in his, and its, history. A taste of the argument that is still going on over this question can readily be gained from the short selection of essays edited by Karl P. Donfried, *The Romans Debate* :[1] there one finds the views that this letter was primarily written to the church at Ephesus (T. W. Manson), or that Paul knew very little of the situation in the Roman church and wrote what he wrote more in the light of his own situation and of his reflections upon his previous arguments with his churches in Galatia and Corinth (G. Bornkamm), as well as the view that Paul is more interested in what he is going to say on his impending visit to Jerusalem (J. Jervell), or that we should assume that Paul wrote to deal with a specific situation in Rome until this should be shown not to be the case (Donfried himself), and others besides.

More recently much the same impression of a prevailing uncertainty on this matter can be gained from the survey of suggestions offered which is given by Dieter Zeller in one of the latest in the series of Romans commentaries that steadily flow from the presses. He mentions for a start the view of Günter Klein (also translated in Donfried's volume) that Paul is seeking to establish a properly and apostolically founded church in Rome; yet Zeller rejects this, for clearly Paul regards the Roman Christians as indeed Christians. Nor, in his view, are the conflicts between the 'weak' and the 'strong' in chapters 14 and 15 an

1

explanation for the letter (*pace* H. W. Bartsch and W. S. Campbell), for Paul is defending, not Jewish Christians (the identification postulated for the 'weak'), but the people of Israel against the arrogance of gentile Christians. Nor is it enough to see him as contending solely against the exclusive claims of Jews (but contrast F. C. Baur, O. Kuss and A. Suhl), for that is equally one-sided. Nearer the truth for this scholar is the suggestion that Paul's previous struggles and his present position explain the polemics of Romans: he resists antinomianism because of his experiences with the Corinthian church, and not because of Jewish-Christian accusations (so Campbell, J. W. Drane and B. N. Kaye), but yet he deals with Jewish Christian opponents too (3.8), which supports the view of Romans as an 'apology' directed towards the Judaizing opponents who dogged his heels (so Kettunen). Against the view of Bornkamm, Jervell and U. Wilckens that Romans was conceived as a speech to be delivered in Paul's defence in Jerusalem Zeller doubts whether the Roman Christians would have spotted the connection between the intercession for the acceptance of the collection which Paul requested of them (15.30-1) and the treatment of Paul's gospel sketched in the letter. Or is it that Paul's visiting card has grown into this impressive document because the Romans were to share in the missionary expansion which he announces in 15.24 (cf. G. Schrenk, Zeller, *Juden* , and Kümmel, 'Probleme')? For the gospel which they were to assist in proclaiming was a controversial one, and one which Paul must justify to himself as well as to others. In the end, however, sure-footed and learned as this account may be, and incisive in its sifting of the various options suggested, the very plethora of suggestions and alternative perspectives offered may leave even the experienced student of Paul with a feeling of frustrated bewilderment.

That there should be so much disagreement over the purpose of Romans is disconcerting in a letter that has perhaps received more learned attention and research than almost any other piece of literature in human history. (It was, after all, the appearance of yet another 'popular commentary' on this letter in particular that provoked one reviewer to wonder whether a 'temporary moratorium' should be declared on such productions;[2] that a commentary on this letter should provoke this comment was no coincidence in view of the steady stream of such works that was flowing out from the presses at that time; and more have appeared since!)

Not that this attention to this single letter is misplaced; far from it. If the influence of Paul's thought on subsequent centuries has been considerable – as it indeed has – then no other letter of his has contributed more to this influence than the Letter to the Romans. This is aptly and eloquently illustrated by F. F. Bruce's article on 'The Epistles of Paul' in the revised edition of *Peake's Commentary on the Bible* : when he wished to point to the significance of these letters and of the role which they had played in Christian history and thought, it was almost exclusively to the influence of this single letter alone to which he turned for his examples – the conversion of Augustine through the words of Rom 13.13*b* -14, that of Luther through his studies of, and lectures on, this letter, and that of John Wesley in turn through hearing the Preface which Luther wrote to it, as well as the impact upon twentieth century scholarship of Karl Barth's commentary on Romans (p. 927).

Yet this same centrality of the letter only makes it the more disconcerting that the circumstances that occasioned the writing of Romans are so disputed. For it has come to be widely recognized that Paul's letters are in large measure to be understood in the light of the context in which they were written. J. Christiaan Beker puts it thus: 'Paul's thought is geared to a specific situation and ... his arguments cannot be divorced from the need of the moment' (*Paul* 25). It follows that to understand what Paul is saying in any of his writings one needs to know as much as possible what that 'specific situation' and that 'need' were. But it is precisely the answers to those questions which are disputed in the case of Romans. It is small wonder, in view of the importance and centrality of the letter in our understanding of Paul, that some scholars try, as we shall see, to make an exception in its case, but it needs to be asked whether such an exception can legitimately be made.

That was recognized as early as 1836 by the great Tübingen scholar, Ferdinand Christian Baur, in an article on the purpose and occasion of Romans. He had to contend with those who treated the letter as a general one, a doctrinal treatise, not rooted in the particular circumstances of the Roman church, an approach which, it will be seen, still has its advocates today. Rightly Baur argued that the onus of proof was on those who thus treated Romans as so different in kind from all the other Pauline letters; if all the other letters of Paul were addressed to a particular situation in the recipients' church, why should Romans be an exception? Paul's grasp of the gospel did not sit there ready-made in his head, waiting to be delivered to the world, but was shaped as he responded to events in the church. Rather 'it is utterly inconceivable that the apostle should have regarded himself as required to write a letter with such contents to this church unless there were certain specific circumstances which obtained in the Roman church, if not exclusively, at least to a greater degree than in any other church' ('Zweck' 68=156). Here he must have faced a stronger challenge to his message, a challenge which Baur finds in the claim of Jewish Christians in Rome that the gentiles could have no part in salvation until the nation of Israel enjoyed it; this challenge underlies the whole letter, but above all chapters 9-11.

It was recognized in the ancient world that letters were like one side of a conversation,[3] and today the comparison is often even more appropriately made with a telephone conversation, for in that case the bystander can usually only hear one side of the conversation and is left to guess the context and the meaning of what is overheard – often a puzzling and tantalizing business! Moreover we are in the position of overhearing from another room, so to speak, for we cannot see the changes of expression and the other visual signals which often help to convey another's meaning and to interpret his or her utterances. Nor can we, unlike the person at the other end of a telephone line, get information from the tone of voice employed by the partner in the conversation (if the line is good enough to permit that!). In that respect the recipients of Paul's letters were no better off than we are, for he communicated with them in writing. At least they usually had the advantage of oral communication by the bearers of Paul's letters, who must often, if not always, have had some knowledge of the contents of the letters, and may well indeed have been entrusted by Paul with further explanation of, and commentary upon, what he had written. Moreover the recipients usually knew Paul personally, and this was probably true even of some of the Roman Christians, as we shall see.

Thus the modern interpreter of Paul's letters stands there listening to one end of the various conversations which Paul had through his letters with various churches throughout the eastern Mediterranean, and he or she has to guess on the basis of what Paul says all that is being said or done at the other end of the lines, so to speak. If our understanding of what Paul is saying in each of his letters is indeed to a great extent commensurate with our knowledge of the other side of the conversation – i.e. who the recipients of the letters were, what they were saying, doing or experiencing, what they had told Paul or what he had been told about them – and if this knowledge is in the case of Romans either not accessible or is at least disputed, then our understanding of what Paul is saying in Romans is of necessity flawed, uncertain and provisional.

For that reason it is undoubtedly most desirable to achieve as clear an insight as possible into the reasons for Paul's writing in these terms. However, many previous attempts to explain why he wrote Romans have been flawed by being partial or one-sided. For any adequate explanation of the writing of Romans has, in my opinion, to do justice to at least six factors, (1) *both* the letter-frame, the beginning and end of Romans which give it the formal characteristics of a letter, *and* the body of the letter which is contained between that opening and that ending, (2) *both* Paul's situation *and* that of the church to which he was writing, and (3) *both* the fact that Paul's arguments in the body of Romans seem to have Jewish criticisms of his message in mind *and* the fact that at times he plainly seems to be addressing himself to Christians who are not Jews (1.13; 11.13; probably 1.5-6). In doing justice to all of these we shall in fact find that no one, single reason or cause will adequately explain the writing of Romans; rather the explanation

is to be found in a constellation or cluster of different circumstances, each contributing in its own way to the writing of the
letter and thus to our understanding of it; hence I have deliberately
chosen the plural 'reasons' in the title of this study (contrast,
however, Zeller, *Juden* 40).

In the first instance, then, we shall consider, negatively,
examples of partial explanations of Romans which fail to do justice
to all of these six factors together, and shall see something of the
implications of, and problems presented by, such neglect, before
going on, positively, to attempt to do justice to all six in the
following chapters.

1. Romans as a Letter

In the case of the Letter to the Hebrews it has been remarked that
it lacks the customary opening of a letter, although it may end like
one; as a consequence W. G. Kümmel concludes that it 'shows no
epistolary character at all'; rather it is a 'discourse' or treatise
(*Introduction* [2] 397-8). There have not been lacking those who
have in effect treated Romans similarly despite the fact that it
obviously possesses the formal characteristics of a letter, both at
its beginning and at its end.

Thus, for instance, the Reformer Philip Melanchthon in an
often quoted phrase described Romans as a 'compendium of
Christian doctrine';[4] this is hardly satisfactory, for, after all, there
are aspects of Pauline, let alone Christian, doctrine, which are not
covered in Romans, and even more which are only touched on,
but are not developed; there are even important issues handled in
earlier letters, but not discussed here, such as the questions of
eschatology and resurrection dealt with in 1 Thessalonians 4 and 1
Corinthians 15. Yet despite this some commentators and scholars
in the present century have continued to treat Romans as if it were
a doctrinal treatise; Beker accuses both Barth and Nygren of this
(*Paul* 65): the former in his Preface to the first edition of his
commentary states that, although 'Paul, as a child of his age,
addressed his contemporaries', he considers it 'far more important
that ... he veritably speaks to all men of every age' (p. 1); the latter
argues that

to offer as the real explanation of the letter the accidental circumstances, of a more personal character, which supplied the occasion for its writing, does not contribute to the deeper understanding of its contents; but quite to the contrary. ... the epistle ... impresses one as a doctrinal writing, a theological treatise, which is only externally clad with the form of a letter. ... Romans does not deal, or deals only in slightest degree, with the conditions within the Roman congregation. But it is nevertheless a real letter. ... Instead of the special problems of the congregation at Rome, we confront Paul's own life problem (*Romans* 6-8).

Ulrich Luz, too, who had earlier blamed recent attempts to explain Romans on the basis of a particular concrete situation for failing to make sense of the letter as a whole (and especially chapters 1-8, but often also 9-11), argues that Romans differs from all Paul's other letters in being

a coherent exposition of the position which Paul had reached in his disputes with his churches. The subject-matter discussed in it is the key to understanding its structure, not the specific circumstances which occasioned it ('Aufbau' 162-3).

And yet justice should not be done to 1.18-11.36 at the expense of 1.1-17 and chapters 12-16, but to both parts of the letter. Yet the list of those espousing such views as Luz's or similar ones could – regrettably – be extended.[5]

The view of Luz that Romans primarily expounds the conclusions reached in earlier arguments with churches other than that of Rome echoes the conclusions of T. W. Manson and G. Bornkamm in the articles mentioned at the start of this chapter. There the latter describes Romans as Paul's 'testament' (the English translation adds 'last will and' to the title of the article for good measure) – despite the fact that, as Bornkamm grants, in writing Romans Paul plainly did not expect to die, but rather, despite the risks involved in his forthcoming trip to Jerusalem which he mentions in 15.31, he expected to be brought safely to Rome to fulfil his long-held ambition to visit the church there (vv 23-4). Rather, for Bornkamm, Romans is an 'unintended' testament (p. 30) – his last literary achievement, for in fact Bornkamm regards Romans as the latest extant letter of Paul's; and even were any of the other letters later this would not, he argues, alter the character of the letter. For, unlike Manson, Bornkamm denies that Romans is a 'mere report and record of former controversies' in Galatia and Corinth (p. 25); rather

> this great document ... summarizes and develops the most important themes and thoughts of the Pauline message and theology and ... elevates his theology above the moment of definite situations and conflicts into the sphere of the eternally and universally valid (p. 31).

(This detachment of Romans from 'definite situations' is only increased by his belief, expressed in his book *Paul* , that Paul's information about the state of the church at Rome was meagre – p. 89.) Yet does this not raise the question why the Roman church, which Paul had neither founded nor even visited before, should be singled out as recipients of 'this great document'? And after all, if Paul did not intend Romans to be his 'testament' and was not indeed in a position to envisage it as such, then to describe it in this way does not further our understanding of why he wrote it; *we* may regard it as his 'testament', but he could not have.

The term 'testament' could also be one way of describing the **literary form** of Romans, but one which I have argued is inappropriate. It is, however, far from being the only attempt to describe its form, nor is that surprising in view of the amount of interest evinced in recent years concerning the formal characteristics and types of letters in the Graeco-Roman world and the relation to them of the letters of the New Testament and in particular those of Paul.[6] Small wonder, then, that attempts have been made to classify Romans according to the various types of letter current in that period.

One such attempt is Martin Luther Stirewalt's appendix to Donfried's *The Romans Debate* on 'The Form and Function of the Greek Letter-Essay'. He groups together into this category of writings the letters of Epicurus, of Dionysius of Halicarnassus, 'selections from the works of Plutarch', 2 Maccabees and the *Martyrdom of Polycarp*. Klaus Berger, too, sees a particular analogy to the New Testament letters in general in those Graeco-Roman letters in which a teacher writes either to individual pupils or to communities of pupils or even to certain cities ('Gattungen' 1338-9). Yet he recognizes, too, the distinctiveness of Romans, for there Paul does not write as a 'ruler', as it were, to his subjects, but to a church of which he is not the apostle (at least not in the sense that he founded it; but see below), and the tone is correspondingly more that of a more general tractate (ibid. 1334-5).

Stirewalt describes such 'letter-essays' as follows: they were written to particular recipients and on specific subjects; yet they were intended to be read by others apart from the addressees. This class of writings is not as wide as that of the didactic letter, for that classification could include school exercises and other fictional letters which lack a genuine letter setting. This group of writings does have in common, however, the fact that each of them in some way supplements another writing, usually by the same author, or 'substitutes for a work projected by him, and the idea of instruction is presented in the author's purpose to clarify, abridge, aid in memorizing, defend his thesis, recount history' (pp. 176-7). Yet, although clarification or defence of a thesis, in this case the gospel Paul preaches, may be an apt description of at least part of what the apostle is doing in writing Romans, it is by no means clear that this letter is meant either to supplement some other work or to act as a substitute for it; it is at most a substitute, for the time being, for Paul's actual presence in Rome. Anyway, such a proposal does not really explain why Paul chose this moment to write this letter, however much it may look like a more general tractate, to the Roman Christians, nor is it at all certain in this case that he also had a wider audience in view. Moreover to describe it as an 'essay', even with the prefix 'letter-', might prejudge decisions yet to be made about the relation – or lack of it – of its contents to the actual situation of the Roman Christians.

Another attempt similarly to fit Romans into one of the categories of ancient letters is Robert Jewett's description of it as an 'ambassadorial letter' ('Romans'). This he sees as a more satisfactory explanation of its character than either regarding it as a treatise or 'the situational theory' (ibid. 6). And yet it is not a pure example of this type, but a 'unique fusion' of this type with other sub-types like the paraenetic letter, the hortatory letter and the philosophical diatribe. Now it is true that Paul's tone and present situation could well be described as those of an 'ambassador for Christ' (cf. 2 Cor 5.20), but is Romans any more 'ambassadorial' than his other letters? True, the 'ambassador' has in this case yet to set foot in the place where he must present his credentials and presents them in advance, as it were, but it is doubtful whether there was a ready-made model of a letter for such a situation; after all the ambassador would usually present his credentials in person and by word of mouth, and if letters were involved they were written by another on the ambassador's behalf. And anyway, even if there had been such a form of letter, it would hardly do to think that Paul plucked such a form out ready-made from amongst the arsenal of available literary models, for who did this except either those seeking to write exemplary materials to be admired or imitated or their pupils?

These attempts to throw light on Romans by defining its literary form seem to me to underline the appropriateness of John L. White's general advice that we should not have it as our primary aim to establish which category of ancient correspondence is most closely related to the New Testament letters. Similarly we could argue that it will not greatly advance our understanding of Romans to place it within this or that category of epistolary types. Rather, White argues, it is important to treat the New Testament letters as letters, and to establish as best we may the purposes which letters serve and what means ancient writers employed in order that their letters might serve such functions (*Light* 218). He earlier described three broad purposes that letters served – conveying information, making requests, enhancing or maintaining personal contacts with the recipient(s) (ibid. 197). Letters generally might combine one or more of these functions. That is certainly arguably true of Romans, for, although it does not employ precisely those formulaic expressions which he selects as typically employed in Graeco-Roman letters for these three functions, this letter does at various points clearly exhibit all three functions:

(a) Paul is concerned to convey information (cf., e.g. 1.13, 'I do not wish you to be ignorant that ...'; 11.25);

(b) he makes requests (e.g. 15.30; 16.1-2, 17, 19);

(c) he seeks either to maintain or to promote good relations with the recipients, depending respectively upon whether he already knows them or merely hopes to meet them shortly when he visits Rome (e.g. 1.6-15; 16.3-16).

But these are very general observations, and so we still need to ask what information Paul was conveying and, above all, why there is no indication that the Roman Christians had asked him for it nor even that news had reached him of circumstances in the Roman church, in contrast to the situation in the case of a letter like 1 Corinthians. And what requests does he make and, again, why? And we even need to ask what the relations are between Paul and the Roman church in general, and whether they are good ones that are merely to be maintained, or whether they are less favourable than he would desire and so are in need of repair.

But all that presupposes that it is in fact to the Roman church that Paul is writing, and that can no longer simply be presupposed. So this brings us to yet another question to which we must, at least briefly, pay attention, for it is vital for this study: was the Roman church the intended destination of this letter?

2. The Destination of Romans

According to Romans 1.7 the letter is addressed to the church in Rome; the omission of the words 'in Rome' in that verse are, if not accidental, probably to be regarded as 'made in order to show that the letter is of general, not local application' (the explanation given by Bruce M. Metzger, *Commentary* 505, of the reading adopted in the 3rd edition of the United Bible Societies' *Greek New Testament*); possibly this represents the earliest attempt to make of Romans a general letter divorced from a particular historical context.

But even if the letter as we have it in the vast majority of manuscripts is unmistakably addressed to Rome, that fact has not prevented scholars from suggesting that the primary recipients of it, those to whom Paul addresses it in the first instance or those of whom he is really thinking as he writes it, are elsewhere than in Rome. Either such scholars argue that Paul wrote it originally for another church and then sent a copy of it, or of part of it, to Rome, or they argue that while writing it to Rome Paul in fact has his eye on an audience elsewhere.

The prime example of the former interpretation is the essay of T. W. Manson referred to above. The suggestion had been made as long ago as 1829, by David Schulz,[7] that **chapter 16** was directed to the church at Ephesus; that suggestion was made on the basis of the contents of that chapter, but Manson now sought to give both confirmation and precision to that suggestion by using textual evidence, namely the evidence of Papyrus 46. For the manuscript tradition of Romans shows remarkable variation in the position of the doxology of 16.25-7, placing it either in its present position or after 14.23 or in both places or omitting it; Papyrus 46, however, is unique in placing it only at the end of chapter 15; we now know, too, that minuscule 1506 has it at the end of chapters 14 and 15 and does not contain 16.1-23. Manson seized on the evidence of the papyrus as the sole textual grounds for his thesis that Romans had once existed in a 15-chapter form; this, he argues, was the form which Paul sent to Rome and the full 16 chapters were sent to the church at Ephesus in whose midst Paul had worked for a considerable time. Manson initially suggested that Paul wrote Romans 1-15 and sent this letter to Rome, and then had a copy prepared for sending to Ephesus, with chapter 16 added (in Donfried, *Debate* 13); however, in the conclusion of his article, he proposes that Paul in fact works out his statement of the conclusions of his arguments in the controversy that occupied him from the time of 1 Corinthians to that of Philippians 3, and sends it to his friends in Ephesus since he did not intend to visit them on his journey to Jerusalem; at the same time he had the idea of sending a copy to Rome with a statement of his future plans (ibid. 15). Thus Romans becomes primarily a letter to Ephesus and only secondarily to Rome; as a consequence

> Romans ceases to be just a letter of self-introduction from Paul to the Roman church, and becomes a manifesto setting

forth his deepest convictions on central issues, a manifesto calling for the widest publicity, which the Apostle did his best – not without success – to give it (ibid.).

Essentially Manson therefore succeeds in doing the same thing to Romans as the scribes did when they excised 'in Rome' from 1.7 (and in 1.15 in two witnesses): he makes the letter a general statement and one not related to any particular issues in the Roman church, nor, for that matter, to any in the Ephesian church either.

For a long time it has been widely accepted that chapter 16 was indeed not part of the original letter to Rome and there are still those who hold this view (e.g. Walter Schmithals). Yet, on the whole, the pendulum of scholarly opinion now seems to have swung back towards the view that this chapter was part of the letter to Rome; in the German-speaking world the recent commentaries of Wilckens and Zeller regard it as such (cf. also W. H. Ollrog), and in the English-speaking world this is argued in the authoritative study of Harry Gamble on *The Textual History of the Letter to the Romans*. This is of considerable importance to us here, since, if Romans 16 with its extensive list of greetings sent to persons known to Paul, or known of by him, is part of the original letter to Rome, then the supposition that Paul knew little of what was going on in the church there becomes far more difficult to sustain. *Such extensive knowledge of who was in the church there is in itself impressively detailed knowledge of this aspect of the life of the church in Rome and indicates that Paul's lines of communication with it were functioning quite well.*

What are the arguments for and against Romans 16's being part of the letter to Rome? Originally, we saw, the case for an Ephesian destination was made out on the basis of the **contents** of the chapter:

(1) The long list of greetings is unparalleled in Paul's letters; some compare the far shorter list in Col 4.10-18, but, even if that letter were Paul's, the names are chiefly of those who send greetings, not of those who receive them. It was argued that this list is strange if Romans 16 is sent to a church which Paul has not visited, but this might be countered by the argument that this in

fact makes excellent sense as a forging of links with a church where Paul is not known personally to all or even to the majority of the members of that church; the unknown apostle can show them that he is not so unknown after all, at least to some of them, and some of them are not so unknown to him either; the higher the standing and the greater the influence of those whom he knows or knows of, the more influential in gaining the respect and regard of the Roman church this catalogue of greetings becomes; it is a classic example of 'name dropping'! Were chapter 16 addressed to the church at Ephesus the contrast between this long list of greetings and the absence of such greetings to named individuals in letters sent to other churches which Paul had founded and which he had also visited more than once and where he had also worked for extended periods of time would be striking; for there Paul does not single out individuals in his greetings – perhaps because to select only some would be invidious, and to greet all by name would use up too much time and writing materials.

(2) Rom 16.3 greets Prisca and Aquila; we are told in Acts 18.2 that they originally came from Rome, but had, along with other Jews, been expelled from that city by the Roman emperor. Acts, it is true, says 'all' Jews in Rome were expelled on this occasion, but the numbers that would probably have been involved casts doubt on the accuracy of this; Kettunen (*Abfassungszweck* 75) estimates that there were at least 30,000-40,000 Jews in Rome before Claudius' edict, and others put the Jewish population around 50,000; the Roman historian Dio Cassius states that in 41 Claudius deliberately refrained from expelling them because of their numbers (60.6.6), and it is hard to believe that numbers as large as these could easily have been expelled eight years later. Anyhow, Prisca and Aquila came to Corinth where they met Paul and worked with him; subsequently they moved to Ephesus (Acts 18.18-19; 1 Cor 16.19; cf. 2 Tim 4.19). But it is the argument of Wolfgang Wiefel (in Donfried, *Debate* 111), amongst others, that Claudius' measures had been repealed by the time of Nero's accession in 54 C.E. and that Jews then began to return to Rome in great numbers; certainly by the time of writing Romans Paul for his part felt free to visit the city despite the fact that he was a Jew

(was Claudius' ban at least one of the factors that had prevented him visiting Rome earlier? – 1.13; 15.23), and this surely implies that Claudius' measures, if not repealed, were at least no longer in force. So had Prisca and Aquila too returned to Rome by then (probably in 57-58 C.E.)?[8]

(3) Less compelling evidence is the mention of the presence of Epaenetus, the 'firstfruits of Asia', i.e. the first Christian convert in that province or among the first converts there (16.5); even if it would be only too natural to find him in the church at Ephesus, the chief city of the Roman province of Asia, it might also be all the more worthy of mention if he was now to be found amongst the members of the Roman church.

(4) It is surprising that 16.17-20 issues so sharp a warning against troublemakers, since polemics of that sort have earlier been strikingly absent from the letter, but they would conceivably be appropriate in a letter addressed to Ephesus, for Paul could address that church with the authority of one who had worked there. (Yet the fact that they only occur right at the close would surely imply that either the bulk of the letter was indeed directed to another church and another situation or that chapter 16 was originally an independent short letter.) Yet perhaps such a change at the very close of a longer letter is possible, particularly if Paul had, as Gamble suggests (*History* 93-4), penned the last chapter or part of it himself. Moreover, as Markku Kettunen notes (*Abfassungszweck* 71-2), such sharp changes of tone are paralleled elsewhere in Paul's letters (he gives as instances 1 Cor 16.22; Phil 3.18-19; 1 Thess 2.15-16), and Paul's language (quite naturally) tends to become sharper when he turns to deal with troublemakers external to the church to which he is writing.

Paul's acquaintance with, or knowledge of, so many people in a church that he had never visited is not hard to explain. Trade and commerce would have brought him news of the church there and of those in it, particularly its leaders; trade and evangelism would have taken thither many whom he had known in Christian churches further to the East, for business of many sorts took great numbers of people to that city; so the Roman historian Tacitus deprecatingly referred to the arrival of Christianity in Rome by remarking that into that city everything hideous or shameful flowed together from every side (*Ann.* 15.44).

Moreover, although some of the names mentioned in chapter 16 seem, at least at first sight, to point towards an Ephesian destination, others if anything point to a Roman one, as Gamble notes, following J. B. Lightfoot (*Phil* 175):

(1) The mention of the household of Aristobulus (16.10) was held by Lightfoot to be a reference to the grandson of Herod the Great who lived in Rome; he was a friend of Claudius and, although he was dead by then, his household may well have retained his name, perhaps having been bequeathed to the emperor and having remained as a distinct entity within the imperial household and still known by their former master's name (so Gamble, ibid. 50, and Lightfoot, ibid.). Lightfoot finds it no coincidence that Paul immediately goes on to greet a Jew, Herodion, 'whose name ... we might expect to find among the slaves or freedmen of a distinguished member of the Herodian family' (ibid.).

(2) The household of Narcissus (16.11) may be that of Claudius' former freedman; true, he too had died by then, shortly after his master, but his household also may have been absorbed into the imperial household, not so much by bequest this time as by confiscation.[9]

(3) In a forthcoming study on *Paul and His Converts* Ernest Best argues that Romans differs in certain respects from those letters which Paul wrote to churches in which he had himself evangelized: he does not call on the readers to imitate him, which is readily intelligible if most of them had never seen him. He avoids the parent/child imagery, presumably because they were not his 'children', so to speak, and does not call them to obey him, but rather to obey Christ and the gospel. He never reminds them of things which he has taught them previously. His more frequent use of the 'diatribe' style (see chapter 3 n. 2 below) with its imaginary interlocutors is particularly appropriate in a letter to a church which he does not know, for elsewhere he can argue directly with his readers (150-1; but compare Schmeller, *Paulus* esp. 407-8).

On the question of the **textual evidence** cited by Manson and mentioned above, it must be noted from the outset that no witness gives direct evidence of a 15-chapter version of Romans, with the possible exception, also noted above, of the minuscule 1506, dating from 1320. But Kurt Aland warns us against seeing this witness as another testimony to the same tradition as Papyrus 46; rather it is a late modification of the 14-chapter version of Romans. Strikingly, Aland notes, the text runs through to 15.33 with 16.25-7 inserted after 14.23, then leaves a half page blank, and then has 16.25-7 once again; the gap seems to indicate that the copyist knew the rest of chapter 16, but decided to omit it ('Schluß' 297). Nor, moreover, is Papyrus 46 direct evidence of a 15-chapter Romans, for the doxology at the end of chapter 15 is followed by 16.1-23.

Certainly the variation in the position of the doxology in the manuscript tradition of Romans remarked on above is most easily explained by postulating the existence of various abridged versions of a Romans that originally contained 16 chapters; a 14-chapter Romans seems to have circulated fairly widely (cf. Gamble, *History* 16-33), and Origen of Alexandria, writing in the third century, attributed such a truncation of Romans to the second century heresiarch Marcion (*Rom* 10.43 in Migne, *PG* 14, 1290AB). It is, however, rather puzzling that Marcion should have found this whole section of Romans in particular especially uncongenial to his theology, if Irenaeus of Lyons is correct in reporting that he removed from Paul's letters all that plainly spoke of the Father of Jesus Christ as the God who made the world, and all that showed the coming of Christ to have been prophesied in the Old Testament (*Haer.* 1.27.2=1.25.1 Harvey). One could think of parts of Romans even more unsuitable in Marcion's eyes if he used these criteria. If 15.8 and 15.25-28 were sufficient reason for Marcion to delete the entire chapter, as Aland argues ('Schluß' 294), then one might have expected little of the letter to have survived his surgery if he had been consistent – but perhaps his consistency should not be assumed. But may it not rather be that, as Gamble suggests (*History* 100-14), Marcion inherited an abridged version of Romans which had already been shortened for

17

other reasons? However Gamble's own suggestion that this abbreviation was part of a catholicizing of the text of Romans is not altogether satisfactory either, for one could imagine that 15.13 or 15.21 would be more appropriate points to insert the editorial knife if one wanted to prune away that part of Romans that spoke to a particular church situation. In other words, none of the suggested explanations of the existence of a 14-chapter Romans seems wholly satisfactory. The deletion of chapter 16 alone, i.e. a text ending at 15.33, could have occurred either as a catholicizing editing or, more simply, as a purging away of what seemed largely a list of names, a purging that took place simply in the name of brevity; after all, some might have found the greater part of that chapter somewhat barren in profound or eminently edifying material. *None of this suggests, however, that either a 14-chapter or a 15-chapter Romans was ever anything but a later, secondary abbreviation of an original 16-chapter letter.*

Yet the nature of this problem is such that these arguments are not, and cannot be, conclusive, but they strongly suggest that it is better to assume that Romans 16 is indeed part of the original letter and that it was directed to the church at Rome. That tells against any theory that the letter originally existed in a longer (16-chapter) and a shorter (15-chapter) version, and it also implies considerable familiarity on Paul's part with the situation in the Roman church.

That brings us to the other possibility mentioned above, that Paul did indeed write Romans to the church at Rome, but that he wrote to them with his eye on a situation elsewhere; that is to say that, although he ostensibly addresses the Romans, the audience whom he in fact envisages in his mind's eye is another one.

Ernst Fuchs argued that it was in fact **Jerusalem** which was the 'secret addressee of the Letter to the Romans' (*Hermeneutik* 191). For M. J. Suggs Romans was 'a brief drawn up by Paul in anticipation of the renewed necessity of defending his gospel in Jerusalem' ('"Word"' 295), and Bornkamm argues that Paul not only writes Romans in the light of his past experiences, but also 'has in mind the impending important meeting with the mother church in Jerusalem and the rounding off of his work as an apostle'

(*Paul* 96). For Ulrich Wilckens too the arguments of Romans are those to be presented in Jerusalem, for which he seeks the Roman church's approval ('Abfassungszweck' 167), but it is clear that primarily he is speaking only of the first eleven chapters. But above all the article by Jacob Jervell in Donfried's *The Romans Debate* announces this by its very title, 'The Letter to Jerusalem'. Jervell asserts that it is 'the major presupposition for an understanding of Romans ... that one frees oneself from the idea that a Pauline letter is primarily determined by the situation of the recipients' (p. 64). Yet that, we may note, is not to say that it then follows that it is not determined *at all* by the recipients' situation. Jervell, however, goes on to assert that

> The essential and primary content of Romans (1:18-11:36) is a reflection upon its major content, the 'collection speech', or more precisely, the defense which Paul plans to give before the church in Jerusalem (ibid.).

So Romans is 'primarily directed to Jerusalem, but also to Rome because Paul needs this congregation', or at least he asked them 'for solidarity, support, and intercession on his behalf' (ibid. 64-5). He is, though,

> not asking support for his future missionary endeavors in Spain. True, he is expressing hope for some aid – probably in terms of food and lodging – so that he will be able to continue his journey after his stay in Rome (15:24). But he is not specifically requesting such aid. Therefore, that is not the reason for his writing; nor would it explain plausibly his extended remarks in the main section, viz., 'first to the Jews and also to the Greeks' (ibid. 66).

He never mentions that he intends to make Rome a base for his missionary work in the West as Ephesus and Corinth served him in the East. Nor is Romans just a summary of what Paul intends to say in Spain – it omits too much of Paul's customary teaching as we know it from other letters. Rather it is concerned with problems that are of particular relevance to Jerusalem. Whereas Galatians dealt with 'justification by faith apart from works of the law' the theme of Romans is that 'the righteousness of God is revealed through faith apart from the law, first to the Jews, then to the Greeks and at the end to all Israel' (ibid. 69). This is not a debate with the Roman church, but it deals with objections which Paul anticipates in Jerusalem. He seeks the aid of the Roman church – a church that belongs to his domain, for he is the apostle to the gentiles; it should be on his side as he goes up to Jerusalem with the collection for the church there.[10]

There is much in Jervell's analysis of Romans that is of great value, but there is one important strand in the letter to which it does not, and cannot, do justice: Paul sides with the 'strong' in faith (15.1) who are apparently able to rise above such legal observances as attaching significance to particular days (14.5) or concern with certain foodstuffs (14.2, 6); the kingdom of God for him too is not a matter of such observances (14.17); the division of food into the ritually 'clean' and 'unclean' is superseded in Christ (14.14). None of these assertions are likely to win approval or favour with the Jewish Christians under James the Just in Jerusalem with their zeal for the Jewish Law (Acts 21.20). But it is in keeping with this identification of himself with the 'strong' who thus discard those sorts of ritual obligations that were the hallmark of Judaism when Paul in 11.13-24 addresses himself to the branches of the wild olive, to use the terms of his image in that passage, who have been grafted on to the stock of the cultivated olive tree; they are, he tells them, not to despise the branches that have been cut off from that cultivated tree, for the latter's very nature fits them even better to be grafted on again. Rather they themselves should take care, for God could even more easily and fitly prune them off too.

Such a line of argument makes no sense addressed to the Jerusalem church, but makes excellent sense addressed to the Roman church and to what is, as we have seen, a predominantly gentile church. That they need to have this warning given to them will, however, also be of considerable significance when we come to evaluate the situation with which Paul is dealing in the Roman church.

But first it is appropriate to look at Paul's situation when he wrote Romans before we consider that of the Roman church, for the former is more generally agreed both to be more clearly described in Romans and to be relevant to our understanding of the letter.

II

PAUL'S CIRCUMSTANCES

Thanks largely to the information with which Paul provides us in chapter 15 of Romans we are in a position to locate the writing of the letter fairly precisely within the sequence of events of Paul's ministry. For there he tells the Romans that he has completed the preaching of the gospel, sweeping round from Jerusalem to Illyricum (15.19),[1] and is now on the point of going up to Jerusalem to present to the church there the financial aid raised for them by the churches of Macedonia and Achaea (15.25-6). He hopes, when that is done, to visit them at last *en route* to missionary work in Spain (15.24, 28), and thus to fulfil a desire that he has long cherished, of seeing the Roman Christians (15.23; cf. 1.10-13).

Whether or not Paul ever got to Spain remains a matter for some doubt; certainly Paul seems to have arrived in Rome under rather different circumstances to those which he envisaged when writing Romans, for, if there is any truth in Acts' account at all, he arrived there not as a free person, but as a Roman prisoner. Whether he was subsequently released we do not know, but it seems somewhat unlikely. His letter to the Philippians may be written from Rome, although very many scholars doubt this; such a setting for the writing of Philippians would, however, give a natural interpretation to Phil 1.13 *if* it means 'amongst all the praetorian guard',[2] and above all to 4.22, 'those of Caesar's household'. Yet if this letter were written from Rome then Paul's hopes were by this time to travel eastwards again and to see the Philippian church if and when he was released (Phil 1.26-7; 2.24), rather than to proceed further west to Spain. Again, little value can be placed with any certainty on the account of Paul's activities, movements and plans given in the Pastoral Letters, but they also give no evidence of either activity or even planned activity in the West.

But, those future plans apart, Paul's movements at the time of writing Romans and in the more immediate future seem to correspond quite neatly with the account given in Acts of his travels in the period just before his final and nearly fatal visit to Jerusalem, described in Acts 21. Of course it is true that, whereas the gathering of the collection to aid the Jerusalem church features prominently in a number of letters of Paul which can be assigned to this period of his ministry, and was obviously much on his mind at this time (cf. not only Romans 15, but also 1 Cor 16.1-4 and 2 Corinthians 8-9), Acts is strangely silent about this project; at most it is alluded to in Paul's speech before Felix in Acts 24.17, but there, if we only had the text of Acts to go by, we would think that Paul was referring merely to a personal gift of 'alms and offerings' to his people presented on his own behalf alone, instead of to what we shall see was probably a collective, communal enterprise of considerable symbolic significance in the eyes of Paul and quite probably of others too, including his critics and opponents. However, reading Acts in the light of Paul's letters, we can make better sense of Acts' mention in 20.4 of a small party which accompanied Paul on this, his last (as far as we know) journey to Jerusalem, the journey which lies before him as he writes Romans.[3] For in 1 Cor 16.3-4 he mentions the procedure which he envisages for the gathering of the collection, including the plan that the Corinthian church should pick delegates to take the money raised to Jerusalem; at that stage he leaves it open whether he himself would accompany them, but evidently later, when he comes to write Romans, he has made up his mind to do so. The absence of any explanation of this party, as well as the unfamiliarity of some of the names mentioned (Sopater and Secundus are not mentioned elsewhere in the New Testament), are perhaps as good evidence as any that at this point the author of Acts is relying upon traditional material, the full significance of which he either may not grasp or may not wish to communicate to his readers; the latter might seem a surprising alternative, were it not for Acts' silence about the collection generally; this is despite the fact that much of the subsequent narrative of the journey to Jerusalem is written in the first person plural (20.5-15; 21.1-18), and this phenomenon in the text of Acts is perhaps most easily and convincingly explained by supposing that the author of Acts, or at least of *an* edition of that work, or a source used by him or her,[4] actually participated in the events thus described. As we shall see, the explanation for this silence may well lie in the failure of the collection; this would almost certainly have been an embarrassment to the author of Acts in view of the implications which it would have had for Paul's gentile mission.

It is customary to assign the writing of Romans to Paul's three-month stay in 'Greece' mentioned in Acts 20.2, and to define 'Greece' more precisely as Corinth, the chief city of the Roman province of Achaea, and the only place where we know of Paul's founding a church in that province. That assumption would be confirmed if the Gaius mentioned in Rom 16.23 as Paul's host and that of the whole church is the same Gaius as is mentioned in 1 Cor 1.14 as one of the few Corinthian converts whom Paul himself baptized; but Gaius is an all too common name – Acts 20.4 mentions a Gaius who according to most manuscripts is from Derbe, and 19.29 another from Macedonia.[5] It would also be confirmed if the Erastus, the city treasurer (*oikonomos*), also mentioned in Rom 16.23 is the same man of that name who provided a pavement in Corinth at his own expense.[6] These identifications are far from certain, but it is clear that to set Romans at about this point in Paul's travels fits all the evidence which we have and seems to be contradicted by none. Equally, however, Alfred Suhl has made out a relatively strong case for Paul's having written Romans from Macedonia (*Paulus* 264-7).

However that in turn raises the question whether all of Romans was in fact written at this point of time. That question must be faced, since it has been argued that it was not, but rather that different bits of it stem from different letters written at different times. If true this would mean that we must seek the reasons for the writing of each of these individual original pieces separately.

1. The Unity of Romans

The unity of Romans 1-15 is assumed by most scholars, but has been challenged by Walter Schmithals in his *Der Römerbrief als historisches Problem*. For him the main body of our Romans in fact contains the contents of two letters plus certain other fragments; these two letters he designates letters A and B. Letter A consists of 1.1-4.25; 5.12-11.36; 15.8-13, and it was sent by Paul from Ephesus in an effort to achieve what he had wanted to accomplish by a personal visit, namely to form the Christians at Rome, former 'God-fearers' or gentile adherents of the Jewish synagogue who still as Christians preserved their former ties with the synagogue, into a Pauline church, espousing his gospel which offered salvation without the obligation to keep the Jewish Law; such a church would serve as a basis for his projected operations in the West. Letter B consists of 12.1-21; 13.8-10; 14.1-15.4a, 7, 5-6; 15.14-32; 16.21-3; 15.33 (in that order). It was written later, when letter A had achieved its purpose and Paul could address a Pauline church which his earlier letter had called into being. Paul was now about to set out on his final journey to Jerusalem (i.e. the point of time usually given for the writing of the whole of Romans), but must call upon his new followers to exercise understanding towards those of their brothers, the 'weak in faith', who are still bound to the synagogue and to at least some of its regulations. These two letters were later edited together, with certain other pieces of material, to form our Romans.

This reconstruction has certain weaknesses. In the first place there is the basic difficulty with all such reconstructions of explaining how and why the two Roman letters were ever joined together in such a fashion. It needs to be explained *how* this happened since, as Aland has remarked ('Entstehung', especially 349-50), it would be most surprising if these separate original letters had left no trace whatsoever upon the manuscript tradition of the Pauline corpus of letters; no trace can be found, and this could only be explained by saying that the editing of these letters to form our present Romans (or any other letter for which such theories of editing are proposed) took place before any copies were made of the original shorter letters and they were sent to other churches; had that happened the chances are that some trace would have been left in the extensive but variegated manuscript tradition. Moreover the same process must have been repeated in all the other churches which are also supposed to have received shorter letters which were then similarly edited and fitted together to form the longer extant letters which we know.

It also needs to be explained *why* such an editing process took place. For, in general, the proponents of such hypotheses of earlier shorter letters being combined to form longer ones appeal in support of their theories to the evidence of contradictions within our present longer letters and of awkward joints and transitions between one part of their text and another. Yet that in turn raises the question why anyone should have wanted to edit these original shorter, presumably more coherent, letters so as to form longer ones with all their tensions and unevennesses. For, in the case of Romans at least, the postulated editing is quite complex, as can be seen from the fragmented nature of Schmithals' letter B especially and from the alterations in the sequence of passages in it compared with our Romans.

Quite apart from these general questions about such theories, the evidence upon which Schmithals builds his case with regard to Romans is open to other interpretations. Principally he bases his case upon two observations:

(1) In chapter 1 Paul is still prevented from coming to visit Rome, but in chapter 15 plans are in hand to realize his ambition to visit them; the impediment to his visit has been removed in the interval between the two letters.

(2) In chapter 15 he declares it to be his policy not to preach where Christ is already known or 'named', for he will not 'build on another's foundation' (15.20); thus he merely wishes to visit the Roman church in passing (15.24); in chapter 1, however, he speaks of preaching the gospel in Rome despite the fact that there are already Christians there (1.15). Paul, Schmithals argues, could

not be thus inconsistent within one and the same letter, but it is easier to conceive of his saying these two different things in two different letters separated by a period of time.

The first point would have been more convincing had Paul not stated in Rom 1.13 that he ' *was* prevented' (aorist) from visiting Rome; the past tense is perfectly compatible with his no longer being thus prevented.

The second point is more difficult. In the first place we have to note the awkwardness of Paul's situation in chapter 1: he writes to a church which he has not visited, yet for which he feels responsible, since they too are among the gentiles and he is apostle to the gentiles (1.5-6). However he cannot, as we shall see, assume a ready hearing; he and his message are suspect in some circles. Thus he at first seems to go to great pains to avoid seeming to impose his authority upon the Roman Christians: rather than a one-way process in which he will impart a 'spiritual gift' to them, he carefully stresses that this will be a two-way process in which both he and the Roman Christians will be enriched by each other's faith (1.11-12). Yet despite this careful qualification of his intended relation to them he apparently speaks of preaching the gospel to them too. Thus there seems to be a considerable tension even within chapter 1; if this reading of the text is correct (and we shall see below that Kettunen advances a different interpretation of Paul's words here), this tension would perhaps be best explained by the existence within Paul's mind of two competing attitudes towards the Roman Christians: he feels responsible for exercising his apostolic ministry among the gentiles there too, but he knows that he must move circumspectly where his authority and rights as an apostle are not recognized.

In chapter 15, on Schmithals' theory, no further preaching is necessary in Rome, for Paul has done what is necessary at long range, by letter (although it is doubtful whether that means of proclamation is any less an infringement of the principle of 15.20 than preaching in person; this is presumably what Klein, 'Purpose' 36, means when he notes a contradiction between 15.15 and 15.20 – cf. Lipsius, *Röm* 85, 196). A church loyal to himself has been called into being. Yet, if that is so, then Rome is, as

Schmithals argues against R. A. Lipsius (*Röm* 85, 195), no alien territory, but now part of Paul's sphere of work. Yet that surely suggests that one reason why Paul should not evangelize in Rome has been removed, at least in one sense: the church there which he now addresses is not built on 'another's foundation'. Why does he then just pass through it? Because Christ is already 'named' there? But Christ was already 'named' there at the time when he wrote his first letter. If anything one might rather have expected Paul to declare his readiness to preach the gospel at Rome also in his *second* letter. Yet, whatever we say, the inconsistency seems to remain, and we have to ask whether Schmithals is right to chide Jervell with preserving the integrity of the letter at the expense of the integrity ('consistency' would surely be an apter term) of the apostle. *Is* it so inconceivable that the apostle whose varied and hardly reconcilable statements about the Jewish Law have been so acutely analysed by Heikki Räisänen in his *Paul and the Law* should be guilty of inconsistency in this matter too? Or is it simply that Paul does not regard the Roman church as built upon a foundation laid by any other particular Christian worker? It may well have arisen simply through the migration thither of Christians from other parts of the Graeco-Roman world and through the witness of those individuals. In that case at no point would his principle enunciated in 15.20 have precluded him from evangelizing in Rome on the grounds that another worker had laid the foundations of the church there; Christ's being named there should have meant that he did not need to preach the gospel there, however, and we must grant a measure of inconsistency in that respect. That was not his point anyway in that immediate context; he simply wished to explain the rationale that lay behind his pioneering work between Jerusalem and Illyricum.

So far we have concentrated on the question whether preaching at Rome would be contrary to Paul's resolve not to 'build on another's foundation'; perhaps Rome would not count in his eyes as 'another's foundation'. But it was still somewhere where Christ was 'named'. To meet that objection Kettunen has made an interesting suggestion: in 1.13-15 Paul is speaking of his earlier ambition to preach in Rome before the church there had come into being. Hence the aorists of v 13, and hence another aorist should be supplied in v 15: it had been his desire to preach the gospel in Rome too. But not just in Rome, but 'to you'. That 'you' surely refers to the Roman Christians, not just to the inhabitants of Rome in general, and there is a certain awkwardness in the idea that Paul would preach the gospel amongst those who were already Christians or that his ministry would bear fruit amongst them. But if Paul is referring to something that he would have liked to have done for them before they had become Christians then his language is the more intelligible (cf. *Abfassungszweck* 118-25, 137-8).[7] This may well be to press too much on Paul's words, but it is an interpretation worthy of serious consideration.

So, whether Paul is merely inconsistent or whether there is an explanation of his words which removes this charge from him, the evidence upon which Schmithals rests his case for the composite nature of Romans and the different settings of its constituent parts is too slender; more convincing reasons are surely needed before we resort to the complex theory of editing which he proposes. We should rather work on the assumptions that all of Romans is to be located at one point of time, and that chapter 15 therefore gives a clear indication roughly when within Paul's ministry the whole letter was written.

2. Paul's Past Struggles

By the time of his writing Romans Paul's controversies, both with the Corinthian church, reflected in 1 Corinthians, and with those who had come into that church to preach another Jesus, as he saw it (2 Cor 11.4), as reflected above all in 2 Cor 10-13, and also with those who preached a 'different gospel' in the Galatian churches (Gal 1.6), all lay in the past. How far in the past they lay is uncertain and depends to some extent on the order in which these three letters (1-2 Corinthians, Galatians) or their constituent parts, if one holds that any of them is composed of more than one letter or of parts of more than one letter, are placed relative to one another; in particular, is Galatians to be dated close in time to the end of the Corinthian correspondence, for its tone and polemic

29

have many points of contact with those of 2 Corinthians 10-13? Or is it earlier than 1 Corinthians? The latter seems in fact more likely, since, by the time of the writing of 1 Corinthians, the Galatian churches have evidently received explicit instructions from Paul concerning the gathering of funds for the collection which he is raising for the Jerusalem church (1 Cor 16.1). It is true that some have seen a reference to this same fund-raising process in Gal 2.10, but it is doubtful whether this mention of a past agreement at Jerusalem to 'remember the poor' is a sufficiently explicit reference to the present gathering of this collection to make it plausible that we should understand the Galatian churches already to be in the midst of gathering the collection. And in view of the ease with which the collection could be misrepresented, in particular as a sign of Paul's subordination to Jerusalem (but cf. also 2 Cor 8.20-1), an especially damaging interpretation in the light of his obvious efforts to show his independence of that mother-church in Gal 1.11-2.14, it is hard to believe that he could have passed over this project in so allusive a fashion as would then be the case in 2.10.

Yet, however we place these letters in relation to one another, they are all earlier than Romans, and the experiences which they reflect lie in the more or less immediate background to Paul's writing of this letter. We have seen how scholars like Bornkamm regard Romans as the product of reflection upon these experiences. Michel, too, begins his commentary on Romans with the observation that

> Unlike Galatians Romans was not written because of a particular situation in the church, but is an expression of a theological insight that has been spawned by arguments with Judaism and Hellenism. (*Röm* 2 n. 1)

It would be surprising if these experiences had not given Paul cause to reflect upon them and if this reflection had borne no fruit in his thinking. But is it then the case that the practical exhortations and instructions contained in the second part of Romans are 'a general paraenesis', as Drane argues ('Paul' 220), rather than being related to any actual specific needs of the Roman Christians? Is it true, for instance, that the injunctions to the 'weak

THE REASONS FOR ROMANS

in faith' and the 'strong' contained in chapters 14 and 15 are a reworking of **1 Corinthians 8-10** or, in the words of Victor Paul Furnish which Drane quotes, 'a generalized adaptation of a position he [Paul] had earlier worked out respecting an actual, known situation in Corinth' (*Love Command* 115; cf. R. J. Karris in Donfried, *Debate*, esp. 94-5; Borse, 'Einordnung' 75-6, goes even further, and sees in far more of the themes of Romans matters that were of relevance in Corinth, but not in Rome)? It will not do, however, simply to cite the range of opinions as to the identities of the 'weak' and the 'strong', as Drane does, as evidence that 'Paul had no specific opponents in view'. (He calls them 'opponents', yet, just because Paul's sympathies are here more with the 'strong', that does not make the 'weak' his 'opponents'; indeed to call them that wholly misses the point of his call for mutual acceptance and tolerance, e.g. in 14.4-13, 22; 15.5-7.) Even if there are 'at least six possible explanations' of these groups, ranging 'from Jewish legalism through vegetarianism to the Hellenistic mystery religions', yet that does not prove that Paul had no particular group in mind. For it is generally agreed that Paul had specific opponents in view when he wrote Galatians, and yet J. J. Gunther lists eight different views as to their identities (*Opponents* 1), as well as a great many more divergent interpretations of the opposition reflected in other Pauline or deutero-Pauline letters. For the weakness of the argument here is that we cannot infer from the fact that the identity of opponents is unclear to us that it must also therefore have been unclear to Paul (or his readers). That is to overlook the gap in time that separates us from him, and the enormous difference between the evidence actually available to us today and the information which was in the hands of Paul and his contemporaries; historical critics ignore this gap and this difference at their peril. What does not make sense or seem apparent to us may well have seemed crystal clear to Paul and his readers.

This lack of consensus as to the nature of the beliefs of these two groups mentioned in Romans 14 and 15 and the variety of different identifications of them does point, however, to the fact that the hints given in chapter 14 as to their respective positions seem surprisingly specific, but at the same time rather surprising in their detail; that they are specific but unexpected is in itself an argument against Paul's statements in that chapter simply being regarded as a matter of a general treatment of 'the same kind of issues of conscience as [Paul] had earlier dealt with in 1 Corinthians 8-10' (Drane, ibid.). Whereas those chapters of 1 Corinthians were dealing with the issue of the eating of food that had been offered to idols, as well as other questions relating to the possibility of Christians' participation in pagan rites, there is no suggestion that this question is being dealt with in Romans. When the food eaten is specified it is just the eating of vegetables by the 'weak' (14.2) and the eating of meat as such, presumably by the 'strong' (14.21), without any mention of the question of the meat's having associations with idolatry. Also at issue is the drinking of wine (14.21; cf. 14.17), and the observance of certain days (14.5). 1 Corinthians 8-10 is addressed to 'those who have knowledge', not to those who are 'weak' or whose conscience is 'weak'; Romans 14, too, primarily addresses the 'strong' and urges them to respect the beliefs of the 'weak' (the very use of this label surely in itself reflects the disparaging viewpoint and attitude of the 'strong), but it also mentions the reciprocal obligations of the 'weak' to respect the position of the 'strong'. This reciprocity is lacking in 1 Corinthians 8-10.

It is surely significant that when the call of Rom 14.1 for acceptance of the 'weak in faith' and the appeal of 14.13 that neither the 'strong' nor the 'weak' should condemn each other are picked up by the summary appeal for mutual acceptance in 15.7, Paul follows that appeal by mentioning Christ's ministry benefiting both the Jews, 'the circumcision', and the gentiles (15.8-9).[8] That makes best sense if the 'you' whom Christ has accepted and who should therefore accept one another according to 15.7 comprise both Jews and gentiles. In turn that suggests that the hindrance to that acceptance comes from the Jewishness of the former and the non-Jewishness of the latter. Furthermore, the fact that many have seen in 14.14 *a* an echo, if not probably an actual or deliberate quotation, of the sort of teaching put on Jesus' lips in Mk 7.14-23 points in the same direction, for there it is the ritual prescriptions of the Jewish Law that are being discussed.

That being so, it seems likeliest that the observance or non-observance of days that is mentioned as a bone of contention in 14.5 concerns Jewish holy days, sabbaths and festivals. But then what of the questions of eating vegetables or meat and of drinking or not drinking wine?

Normally Jews ate meat of certain kinds as long as the animals had been correctly slaughtered, and normally they did not regard wine as forbidden, even if they were normally only accustomed to drink it on special, festive occasions (Jeremias, *Words* 50-2). But sometimes in pagan surroundings it was different: it is instructive that Daniel 1 tells of Daniel and other noble Jewish youths at the court of Nebuchadnezzar abstaining from 'the king's rich food' and wine,⁹ and instead eating only vegetables and drinking water (Dan 1.12, 16). That suggests that in certain circumstances, in pagan surroundings, a pious Jew might feel it to be his or her duty to adopt a vegetarian diet and to abstain from wine.

The Therapeutae too, whom Philo of Alexandria describes and praises in his treatise *On the Contemplative Life*, avoided both the flesh of animals and wine (§§73-4); they too were a group of Jews living in a pagan world, by the Mareotic Lake near Alexandria (§22). Whereas Daniel tells of a Jewish group in the pagan royal court, where ritually pure meat could not readily be obtained, Philo describes a relatively self-contained community who could presumably, had they so wished, have procured themselves ritually pure meat and wine, yet did not do so and avoided such food and drink. Philo compares their avoidance of wine with the abstinence of priests when sacrificing,¹⁰ and this may suggest that their practice in this respect was like that of a permanent priesthood. It may be significant too that behind Colson's translation '(the table ... is kept pure from) the flesh of animals' lies a Greek word meaning 'that which has blood in it' (*enaimos*); this could merely mean that they abstained from meat that had not had the blood drained from it in accordance with ordinary Jewish ritual requirements, but if indeed Philo means us to understand that they abstained from *all* meat (and he does go on to mention the bread which they ate as an alternative) then this might simply be a matter of taking the usual Jewish avoidance of blood a stage further, by avoiding all meat because it had had contact with blood. Whatever their reasons this points to the possibility of Jewish groups in the Diaspora of an ascetic disposition who avoided both flesh and wine.

There may be further evidence of this in the *Testament of Isaac* which its editor and translator in J. H. Charlesworth's *Old Testament Pseudepigrapha*, W. F. Stinespring, assigns to the second century C.E., but which he thinks stems originally from Egyptian Judaism (1, 903-4); here we find that the patriarch Isaac is a life-long abstainer from meat and wine (4.5), as well as from fruit (4.6); he is, moreover, sparing in his consumption of bread as well (4.41).[11]

Especially interesting here, because it concerns certain Jews in Rome in the time when Felix was procurator of Judaea (approximately 52-60 C.E.;[12] i.e. he was procurator at the time when Paul wrote Romans), is an account in Josephus' *Life* (§14): certain priests whom Josephus knew were sent to Rome as prisoners by Felix to be tried by the emperor; Josephus heard that

> even in affliction, they had not forgotten the pious practices of religion, and supported themselves on figs and nuts (tr. Thackeray).

If such ascetic groups existed in Diaspora Judaism, it is plausible and indeed likely that Christians too, who retained links with Judaism, may well have shared these traits if they were prevalent in the Judaism with which they were in contact; certainly this ascetic example was followed by later Christian groups.[13] All in all this seems the likeliest explanation for the otherwise rather puzzling series of practical examples of contrasting attitudes to the Christian life which Paul gives us in Romans 14.[14]

In short the information given in Romans 14 can be fitted coherently into a situation in which Christians are involved who were disposed to adopt a rigorous, ascetic form of Jewish practice. These formed at least part of the ranks of the 'weak', who might well also have included Christians adopting a less rigorous form of Jewish observance. If so, then the distinction between the 'weak' and the 'strong' here seems to have a very different basis and character to that in 1 Corinthians 8-10, where the 'weakness' of the 'weak' seems to come, not from their affinities to Judaism, but from their previous associations with idolatry: they have been accustomed to eat food offered to idols as something connected with idolatry (1 Cor 8.7). Moreover 1 Cor 9.20-2 implies that the category of the 'weak' was different from either those of the 'Jews' or of 'those under the Law' (which are probably not coterminous either; for the latter could include gentiles who kept the Jewish Law or part of it, and not all Jews were 'under the Law', for Paul and others were not – Rom 6.14) or of 'those without the Law'; this separate category of the 'weak' is the more intelligible and necessary if Paul was primarily thinking in 1 Corinthians of former pagans who retained many of the beliefs and scruples of their pagan past. In that case, whatever the analogies between Romans 14 and 1 Corinthians 8-10, there are marked differences in the situations presupposed; but at the same time both, it may be suggested, are quite specific situations, and neither is a hypothetical generalization or simply an extrapolation from the other.

In other words, although Paul's past struggles with the Corinthian church have undoubtedly contributed to the development of his thought, and have therefore left their mark on his statements in Romans, that letter has reshaped the fruits of those experiences in such a way that it is hardly intelligible unless a fresh situation has arisen to which Paul responds creatively in Romans (cf. Williams, '"Righteousness"' 253-4). The theme may be similar, but we also have to explain the variations, and it is surely implausible to imagine Paul simply sitting down to dream up fresh situations to which he might apply the insights gained in his arguments with his Corinthian converts, especially situations that are delineated so specifically and are so untypical as to have caused so much searching after even approximately parallel practices.

Can one then say that Romans is simply a reworking of the themes of **Galatians**? To some extent it is true that, as Wilckens observes ('Abfassungszweck' 143; cf. 167), 'Romans is ... a repetition of Galatians' in the light of the demands of Paul's present situation and in the light of further fresh reflection. Some of the themes of Romans are ones dealt with in Galatians, and they are dealt with in different ways. This has even led Enslin to toy with the idea that Romans as a whole was addressed to the Galatians, although he ends by preferring to see it as actually sent to several churches (*Reapproaching Paul* 108-9). Yet there are matters handled in Galatians which are not dealt with in Romans and *vice versa*. Romans, for example, has no equivalent to the long autobiographical section of Galatians, 1.11-2.14; Galatians lacks any equivalent to the sustained argument of Romans 1.18-3.20 to show that 'all sinned and lack God's glory' (3.23). Sometimes the themes common to the two letters are dealt with so differently that it is less than helpful to call the one letter a 'repetition' of the other. Both letters, for instance, treat Abraham as an example of justification by faith, quoting Gen 15.6 (cf. Rom 4.3; Gal 3.6). Galatians, however, concentrates very much on the relation of the promise given to Abraham to the later giving of the Law, and on the promises's being made to Abraham and his seed (3.6-4.7); Romans ignores these arguments and instead investigates the nature of Abraham's faith and its relation to his later circumcision (chap. 4). Thus Beker rightly observes, in a detailed comparison of these sections of the two letters, that

> although both ... interpret salvation-history, Galatians 3 focuses on the principles that constitute that history, whereas Romans 4 centers on the existential stance of Abraham's personal faith as example for all believers (*Paul* 98).

He goes on to observe that Galatians stresses the discontinuity of that salvation-history, disrupted by the intrusion of the Law, while Romans stresses its continuity, with Christians' faith being foreshadowed and exemplified in that of Abraham. And those differences, he rightly notes, stem from the different situations and different audiences addressed in the two letters (ibid. 99-100). Thus to point to such similarities between these letters may do little more than remind us that the same person wrote both of them, and that his mind and way of thinking has not utterly changed in the interval between the writing of them; he writes the second letter, Romans, in the light of the experiences reflected in the earlier letter and of his responses to them then. But that is far from being the whole story, and it still remains to be shown why

Paul takes up such themes, but handles them and uses them in two such different ways. In other words he also writes in the light of experiences that he has had since writing Galatians, and in the light of a new situation that has arisen, both as regards himself and his own position, and also, arguably, in the church to which he now writes.

3. The Collection and Paul's Visit to Jerusalem

One part, one very important part, of that new situation in which Paul finds himself in writing Romans is his impending visit to Jerusalem with the collection, the aid gathered for the Jerusalem church in the churches which he had founded.[15] At the time of writing Galatians, it was argued above, the plans for gathering the collection had not yet been set in motion. At most Gal 2.10 may indicate that the possibility of such a project was in his mind.

Of course, some reconstructions of Paul's ministry place the agreements reached in Gal 2.1-10 immediately before the period in which Paul was engaged in raising the collection and then conveying it to Jerusalem.[16] These theories, which set the meeting of Gal 2.1-10 at that point of time represented by the cryptic reference to Paul's going up to 'greet the church' in Acts 18.22, i.e. after both the first two missionary journeys of Paul recounted in Acts 13.1-18.22, do have the great merit of leaving no gap between the agreement to remember the poor recorded in Gal 2.10 and the implementation of that agreement in the collection-project. However they do also present problems: that of Acts' apparent trivializing of so momentous a gathering in 18.22 is not so serious; the author of Acts may simply have known of a series of visits by Paul to Jerusalem and have picked the wrong one as the setting for this meeting which had such far-reaching implications for the mission of the Christian church, placing it on the occasion of an earlier visit (in Acts 15). It is more difficult to explain then Barnabas' association with Paul in Gal 2.1, 9, since Acts seems to imply that they parted company, as the result of a personal disagreement, in Acts 15.39-41, before the second missionary journey. In Galatians, however, their views, and presumably also

their ways, diverge only in Gal 2.13, although the disagreement
there is of a far more fundamental and serious nature than that
mentioned in Acts, for it affects the very constitution and nature
of the Christian church: Barnabas was persuaded to break with his
previous practice of eating with gentile Christians. These considerations suggest that the meeting of Gal 2.1-10 took place earlier,
before the second missionary journey (Acts 16.1-18.22) and
indeed possibly even before the first (Acts 13-14).

Yet, if the agreement of Gal 2.10 is the basis of the collection,
why was Paul then so long in implementing it? For he would then
have allowed either one or two missionary journeys to intervene.
The first thing to note here is that it was in fact the Antioch church
which undertook the responsibility 'to (continue to) remember
the poor',[17] and Paul very likely had relatively little to do with that
church after the quarrel recorded in Gal 2.11-14; at any rate his
partnership in mission with Jewish Christian leaders of that
church like Barnabas would have become impossible. The other
thing to note is the suggestion by Dieter Georgi (*Geschichte* 33)
that Paul implies that the terms of the Jerusalem agreement of Gal
2.1-10 had already been broken by the activities of the 'certain
people that came from James' and provoked the quarrel in
Antioch of 2.11-14 by demanding that Jewish Christians and
gentile Christians should not eat together. It is true that the
different sides to that agreement may have seen its terms
differently. It did recognize the legitimacy of the Antioch church's
mission to gentiles: they could admit gentiles to the church. But
that did not *necessarily* mean that they could then associate freely
with Jewish Christians or that the latter were free to associate fully
with them at the cost of their Jewishness. Perhaps some Jewish
Christians felt that the agreement merely recognized the legiti-
mate existence of two different gospels, or two different versions
of the gospel, i.e. two different messages about the terms upon
which one might obtain salvation;[18] the implicit corollary of that
would be that there would then be two different communities of
the saved, each living according to its own conception of what
God required of them. Yet Paul could also have reasonably felt
that this interpretation ran counter to the spirit of the Jerusalem

agreement, even if it was compatible with the letter of it. And if he felt that the main point of the agreement had been broken, and that he was thus in danger again of having to 'run in vain' (2.2) if he was only to gather together an alternative community of the saved, then it is understandable that he should view the agreement to aid the Jerusalem poor as suspended too. Perhaps that is why he writes that he had been eager to aid them, using a past tense (*espoudasa*, aorist); once he had been keen, but then that had changed.

But then is the collection which he subsequently raised connected in any way with this agreement? Georgi notes that he never appeals to the Jerusalem decisions in connection with his organization of the collection (*Geschichte* 33). Yet the fact that he mentions this aspect of the agreement when writing Galatians is perhaps significant, particularly if we set Galatians near in time to the writing of 1 Corinthians, for by the time of the writing of that letter the preparations for the collection are, as we have seen, in hand, and instructions have been issued to the churches involved.[19] It may confirm the suggestion made at the start of this section that the collection-project was linked in his mind with his awareness of this facet of the Jerusalem agreement.

Yet it is probably right to stress the differences between what was envisaged at the Jerusalem meeting and what Paul was now undertaking:

(1) The Jerusalem agreement was to the effect that the Antioch church should aid the Jerusalem church (as it had once done already according to Acts 11.29), but Paul's plan did not involve the Antioch church, but only those churches which he himself had founded.

(2) The aid mentioned in Gal 2.10 was requested by the Jerusalem church, but the collection was undertaken on Paul's initiative, and, as we shall see, it was by no means certain that it would be welcomed by the Jerusalem church (Rom 15.31).

(3) It is also probably correct to regard Paul's collection as having a symbolic significance which the aid envisaged by the Jerusalem agreement did not. Not only was it a recognition of the spiritual aid that the Jerusalem church had given to the gentile

churches (Rom 15.27), but in all probability it was too, as Georgi also suggests (*Geschichte* 84-6), a sign to Israel; but perhaps it was not so much because it recalled biblical promises of the pilgrimage of the nations to Jerusalem; rather it gave concrete expression to Jewish and gentile Christians' common sharing in the spiritual heritage of Israel (Rom 15.27; cf. 11.17; ?12.13). That was, as we shall also see, a controversial point. It too could provoke the Jews to jealousy just as Paul hoped that the gentiles' salvation (11.11 – fulfilling the prophecy of Moses in Deut 32.21 according to Rom 10.19) and his own ministry (11.14) would. Yet 'jealousy' is a fickle and ambivalent thing: it can either spur the jealous to acquire for themselves that of which they are jealous and which they do not themselves have, or it can provoke them to seek to deny to those of whom they are jealous the possession of that thing which they begrudge them, whether or not they have it themselves. Paul in this instance hoped for the former, positive reaction, but there was a very great danger that the reaction would be largely the latter. Such a reaction nearly cost Paul his life when, according to Acts 21.29, he was suspected of having brought gentiles into those parts of the Jerusalem Temple reserved for Jews; for their holy privileges were not to be shared with unclean gentiles, and woe betide the Jew who sought to abet the gentiles in this intrusion into Judaism's prerogatives. After all this venture fell in the period just after that which Jewett describes as one in which 'Jewish Christians in Judea were stimulated by Zealot pressure into a nomistic campaign among their fellow Christians in the late forties and early fifties' of the first century; he also finds in the plot against Paul mentioned in Acts 23.12-22 (cf. 20.3) slightly later evidence of this menacing 'Zealotic pressure' which was prepared to commit 'atoning murders' of 'those who retained contact with uncircumcised persons' ('Agitators' 205).

Acts, as we noted above, is strangely silent about the collection. Is it too much to suggest that its silence is deliberate, and that this project of Paul's failed because the Jewish Christians clung on to their spiritual privileges too jealously, and refused to accept the offerings that would have symbolized Jewish and gentile Christians' common sharing of their spiritual and material riches (Rom

15.27)? In that case Paul's concern both for his own safety and for the acceptability of the collection, voiced in Rom 15.31, were alike well-founded: he nearly lost his life at the hands of jealous Jews, and the collection was spurned by Jewish Christians jealously clinging on to their spiritual privileges and refusing this *quid pro quo*. That would have been a most damaging rejection of the proffered gift, in the eyes both of Paul and of the author of Acts, for it was tantamount to a denial that gentile Christians had an equal share in the spiritual heritage of Israel. And if gentiles had to become Jews first in order to receive a full share in that heritage, then the whole basis of Paul's Law-free mission was undermined, and Jerusalem's rejection opened the way for Judaizing missionaries, with or without the express encouragement of the Jerusalem church, to enter Paul's churches as they had done in Galatia and probably also elsewhere, and to proclaim there that full salvation was only possible for gentiles if they submitted to the Jewish way of life, either fully or in part.[20]

4. Paul's Present Situation

We have seen that it is possible that Paul writes Romans from Corinth; in the past Paul's relations with the church there had been stormy. Quite apart from the sharp tone of his letters, particularly 2 Corinthians 10-13, he had written them one letter 'out of much affliction and anguish of heart and with many tears' (2 Cor 2.4, *RSV*); although some have thought that at least part of this earlier letter is preserved in 2 Corinthians 10-13, 2 Cor 13.1 seems to presuppose a later situation where Paul is proposing a third visit to Corinth, and so we must probably assume that the letter written with tears has not survived at all, for 2 Corinthians 10-13 does not seem to be what is referred to by Paul; perhaps it was too painful for the Corinthians for them to want to preserve it. Again, as the reference to a projected third visit mentioned above indicates, Paul has paid a second visit to Corinth subsequent to that recorded in Acts 18.1-17, his first visit in which he founded the church in that city. He also mentions what is presumably this same second visit in 2 Cor 2.1 when he refers to a 'painful visit';

41

Acts, however, has left us no record of this visit, again perhaps because it was too painful and embarrassing a rebuff for the author's hero Paul.

Yet Paul makes no mention of troubles in the Corinthian church when he writes Romans, or indeed of troubles anywhere else in his churches, as Kettunen notes (*Abfassungszweck* 139-40). Is that simply because he writes from elsewhere, e.g. Macedonia, as suggested by Suhl, or does it mean that harmonious relations have now been restored between the apostle and his congregation there? Perhaps it does imply that, but, had the situation not been so peaceful, would Paul have found it expedient to mention that surely embarrassing fact when writing to a church where he was not generally known and where there were some present who were disposed to be critical of him and his ministry?[21]

There is one hint that all might still not be well there, and that is in the list in Acts 20.4 of those who set out with Paul from Corinth on the journey to Jerusalem with the collection, a list which, it was suggested above, seems to be a piece of information that the author of Acts has gleaned from somewhere. (And one hint of the existence of such pieces of tradition is often that they either seem to contain details of information that have no particular detectable purpose within the narrative of Acts or that they are in tension with the picture of the church's life which the author seems to wish to paint or both at once.) Although 1 Cor 16.3 envisages delegates from the Corinthian church taking the collection raised in their church to Jerusalem, no delegates from Achaea or Corinth are mentioned in Acts' list. Does that mean that the Corinthian church had finally deserted Paul, lured away by the intruders whom he so bitterly condemns in 2 Corinthians 10-13, and that they had therefore declined to participate in the collection?

However Rom 15.26 does mention the churches of Achaea's decision to participate in the collection, and that might seem to settle the question: Corinth remained true to Paul and backed him in this venture. Yet Acts' list of delegates remains a problem. Is there then any significance in the fact that Paul records their decision in a past tense (*eudokēsan*)? That at least in theory leaves it open whether their decision still held good. Had they changed their mind, or were they still undecided what to do when Paul wrote Romans? In that case the absence of delegates from Achaea in Acts is indeed significant and means that those churches (or that church if only the one in Corinth is meant; but it is likely that at least Cenchreae, the port of that city, had a separate church – Rom 16.1) were also in the end lost to Paul.

If that is so, and it can be no more than a possibility, however strong, then is it not surely all the more remarkable that Paul in such a situation turns his thoughts westwards to Rome and finds the time and the energy to dictate this lengthy letter to the Roman Christians? Or is it that the gathering opposition to him in the eastern churches was a powerful factor in persuading him that he should now seek fresh pastures in the West? He had done his duty in the East (Rom 15.19). In the light of this an added significance would be given to Paul's hope, expressed in 15.32, that his time at Rome might be one in which he experienced comfort and refreshment, as Michel translates *synanapauomai* there (*Röm* 331, 337; cf. Kettunen, *Abfassungszweck* 165). Was it that he hoped for relief from the ravages of his opponents and critics who were undoing his work and frustrating his efforts, and hoped to find some much needed encouragement in the welcome that he hoped to find awaiting him in the Roman church? At least in the far West he might be further from the Jerusalem church, whose emissaries, official or unofficial, had so hampered or undermined his work in the East. But Rome was in many respects the key to future work in the West, for not only did all roads lead to it, but all led out from it as well. A supporting base there would be a great asset, but could he count on that support there? Or was the baneful influence of the Jerusalem church felt there as well? That leads us to the questions of how much we know about the Roman church, and of how much Paul knew, and that in turn to the question of the bearing of his knowledge upon the contents of Romans.

III

THE CIRCUMSTANCES OF THE ROMAN CHURCH

It is manifestly harder to speak with the same degree of certainty about the situation which obtained in the Roman church to which Paul wrote. We have seen that there have been many who have claimed that Paul did not know much about the situation there, or that he was not addressing himself to that situation anyway, but rather writing in the light of another situation, that of himself or of his churches in the East or both. That they can claim such a thing with any plausibility stems from the paucity of any clear information about the Roman church in the letter, particularly if one dismisses chapter 16 as addressed to another church (see chapter 1 §2 above). But the point made in our previous chapter concerning Romans 14 and 15 holds good with regard to the whole letter too: it is generally agreed that Galatians is written to a specific situation, and that Paul knew of that situation. Yet how much do we really know about the Galatian churches? We are even uncertain where they were, whether they were in the south of the Roman province of Galatia or in that area of central Anatolia where the ethnic Galatians lived. We can make more or less intelligent guesses as to the nature of their problems, but scholars differ in their guesses, and in their assessment of the beliefs of those who had infiltrated into those churches. At most they seek to present a historically coherent picture of the situation there, one which is plausible in itself and accords with what we gather was going on elsewhere in the early church. Nevertheless there is not much scope for doubting the reality of the threat to those churches or for denying Paul's awareness of the situation there.

In the case of Romans 14 we saw in the previous chapter that a case could indeed be made out for Paul's familiarity with a quite specific set of circumstances in the Roman church, a set of circumstances markedly different from that in the Corinthian church with which he had dealt in a partially analogous way in 1 Corinthians 8-10. He had learnt from his experiences with the Corinthians, it is true, but the evidence of the text of Romans 14 was more plausibly explained by supposing that Paul was now confronted with a fresh set of circumstances in the Roman church; an account of those circumstances could, we saw, be given which possessed a certain internal coherence, and made sense as an explanation of the situation reflected in that chapter. But how does that account fit into the rest of the picture that we have of the Roman church, if we have any picture at all? What further clues does the letter give us, and what more can we reasonably and plausibly say about the nature of, and situation in, the Roman church?

1. A Divided Church?

If chapter 16 is directed to Rome then we have good evidence for the existence in Rome of more than one Christian house-group: there is a church (*ekklēsia*) in the house of Prisca and Aquila (16.5); the references, too, to those 'with' Asyncritus, Phlegon, Hermes, Patrobas, and Hermas in v 14 and to those 'with' Philologus, Julia, Nereus and his sister, and Olympas in v 15 are most plausibly regarded as indicating house-groups gathered around those named here by Paul. Paul Minear (*Obedience* 7) also adds the family or household of Aristobulus (16.10) and that of Narcissus (16.11). However in the first chapter we saw that the latter reference at least might well simply be to a group of people designated by that name; it need not imply that they met separately as a church. Yet this too would be possible; Wiefel notes the existence of a Jewish synagogue in Rome known as the Augustesians, 'probably consisting of the emperor's freedmen or founded by them', and others bear the names of Agrippa and Volumnius, procurator of the province of Syria in the time of

Herod the Great, and another that of the Herodians ('Community' 106). Members of the households of Aristobulus and Narcissus might also have continued to exist as groups of Christian worshippers in Rome.

A precedent for this division into separate groups of worshippers may quite possibly have been set by the Jewish community in Rome, to which some members of the Roman church may well have previously belonged or indeed still belonged, as we shall see. For that community was also divided into a number of different synagogues, as Wiefel notes (ibid.; cf. Schürer, *History* 3.1, 96-8); inscriptions testify to the various names of these groups, variously called after their founders or the places of origin of their members or in other ways. One could wish that we knew more about these synagogues than the inscriptions tell us; besides their bare names or the titles of their officials which the inscriptions contain it would have been of great interest to know whether they differed in their beliefs and practices or in their adherence to the various different movements within both Palestinian and Diaspora Judaism of that day,[1] but unfortunately of that we learn nothing from this source. Thus we cannot tell whether these various Jewish synagogues differed in practice or belief from one another, or whether their separate existence was dictated simply by such practical considerations as the size of their meeting places or their geographical location or by the force of habit or of traditional ties. We cannot tell whether some were more liberal, others more conservative, or whether any were influenced more or less by any of the different traditions represented within Palestinian Judaism at that time. We do know, however, that their inscriptions were chiefly written in Greek, particularly at the time which concerns us, the first century C.E., and Wiefel reasonably concludes that Greek was the language used in these congregations (ibid.); thus they do not seem to have been divided according to the language which they used.

What of the various Christian groupings? Did they group themselves solely on the grounds of convenience? Did the size of their meeting places or the position of these determine their distribution? Or did they just meet in certain groups through force of habit? Or did they differ amongst themselves in their beliefs and practices, and may they thus have split into different groups because of these various differences and the tensions which they caused? The truth may be that all three sorts of factors, practical considerations, habit, and strife, may have had some part to play.

Minear is one scholar who has argued for the dominant role of disagreements over doctrine and practice in the formation of these different groups; moreover, in the text of Romans he finds Paul addressing himself at different points to five different groups amongst the Christians in Rome (*Obedience* 8-17). These groups are

(1) 'the "weak in faith" who condemned the "strong in faith"',

(2) 'the strong in faith who scorned and despised the weak in faith',

(3) 'the doubters',

(4) 'the weak in faith who did not condemn the strong', and

(5) 'the strong in faith who did not despise the weak'.

He appeals both to the analogy of the various Jewish synagogues and to the evidence of different house-groups within the Christian community in Rome, and argues that the latter 'cells were brought into existence at diverse times, by diverse leaders, with diverse conceptions of the gospel' (ibid. 7). He does not expressly say that there is any exact correlation between the five 'distinct factions' or five 'different positions' which he detects in Romans and the 'at least five or six different house-churches' of which he finds evidence in chapter 16, but the implication lies close at hand.

Few have found Minear's position entirely satisfactory. It will be clear, however, from what has been said earlier that it would be over-hasty to reject his theory out of hand merely on the grounds that Paul was just not that well-informed about the situation in the Roman church, so that he could direct his remarks specifically to these various distinct groups; the thrust of the argument up to this point has been that indeed he may well have been quite aware of it.

Some of the reasoning which supports Minear's reconstruction of the situation in the Roman church is, however, not entirely convincing. Some of the remarks in Romans, for instance, which are supposedly addressed to one or other of these specific groups are in fact formulated in the second person *singular* (e.g. 14.22); this use of the second person is not so much a direct appeal to a particular group (which one would expect to be addressed in the plural, as Paul does when he addresses the whole church in Rome in 1.6-7) as the use of a vivid style of address which many have held to be characteristic of the 'diatribe' or popular philosophical lecture or tract. (Some have cast doubt upon such a comparison with this philosophical material – e.g. Drane, 'Paul' 219-20; however, although 'diatribe' is a name that has been applied to a very wide and diverse body of literature,[2] yet there seems no good reason for doubting that this and other such stylistic devices were a common feature of popular Graeco-Roman philosophical literature of the time.)

It is clear, too, that members of Minear's first two groups might find it difficult to meet amicably in one place, but it is not clear why members of the other three groups could not have met and worshipped and perhaps even eaten together, even if not with wholly easy minds and consciences. To that extent the questions of different house-groups and different 'factions' are separate and distinct. However, it is true that the existence of various groups meeting in different places might enable groups with different outlooks more easily to go their own ways; birds of a doctrinal feather could flock together, and those of a like mind could gravitate towards one another, and would not have to thrash out their differences in regular contact with one another (cf. Drane, 'Paul' 216). We should not, however, treat the existence of separate house-groups as in itself evidence of divisions in doctrine and practice;[3] for that we must look to other signs in the letter of different beliefs and practices, such as those which we have already seen in looking at chapter 14.

It is also questionable whether Paul's failure to address the Christians in Rome as a whole as a 'church' (but the word *ekklēsia* is found applied to a single house-group in 16.5) is evidence of their division (*pace* Bartsch, 'Situation' 330); anyway, Paul elsewhere addressed divided congregations as a 'church' (1 Cor 1.2; contrast 1.11; 11.18). His omission may seem surprising, but may have a more innocent explanation: he just happened not to use it, rather than decided to withhold it. For Kettunen argues that in the proem of Romans (1.1-7) Paul addresses the Romans with 'highly expressive predicates appropriate to the promised people of God' (*Abfassungszweck* 36-7): they are 'called' and 'beloved of God', and these terms echo the quotation of Hosea 2.23 and 1.10 (LXX 2.25; 2.1) in Rom 9.25-6:

> Those who were not my people
> I will *call* 'my people',
> and her who was not beloved
> I will call 'my *beloved* '.
> And in the very place where it was said to them, 'You are not my people',
> they will be *called* 'sons of the living God' (*RSV*).

These verses he quotes immediately after asserting that God has called out his people, not only from among the Jews, but also from amongst the gentiles (9.24). So Kettunen argues that Paul had such texts already in mind when he addressed the Roman Christians at the start of his letter. Moreover, it was not Paul's practice to attach such laudatory epithets as 'called' and 'beloved of God' to the word 'church', but that hardly seems a strong reason for Paul's not doing so here had he so wished. Perhaps rather the use of such a term seemed superfluous and redundant after such eloquent expressions of God's favour and electing grace.

However, as the case of 1 Corinthians indicates, high praise of a church does not mean that all is well in it; such praise can still be offered to one riven with strife. It was argued in the previous chapter that chapter 14 does indeed point to considerable differences of opinion and practice in the Roman Christian community, that Paul has to appeal there for mutual respect and toleration, and that observance or non-observance of the Jewish Law lay at the root of those differences. There seems to be some evidence that this problem had already a considerable history behind it, and to that we must now turn in the following two sections.

2. Judaizing Christianity at Rome

The problem that concerns us here is, then, the evidence for the existence and prevalence of a form of Christianity at Rome that could best be described as 'Judaizing'. The phrase 'Jewish Christianity' has been, and should be, avoided here, since it is, as we shall see below, a notoriously elusive and ambiguous term. Here we are concerned with what might be better and more precisely described as 'Judaizing Christianity', that is a form of Christianity which treats Christianity as simply part of Judaism and, more important, requires of all its adherents, whether they are Jews or not, that they observe the Jewish Law as the Jewish Law either in whole or in part. (They should observe it 'as the Jewish Law' and not just because some of its requirements happen to overlap with the imperatives of some form of the Christian gospel.) In other words the patterns of thought and of behaviour of Judaism are dominant and determinative for the nature of Christianity. 'Judaizing Christianity' is an apter term than 'Jewish Christianity' to describe this form of Christianity, since

(a) it is doubtful whether any Christianity at all existed at this period that was not in some sense 'Jewish', in that it derived its existence from a Jewish founder and also inherited its thought-world from the Jewish matrix in which the Christian movement came into being (and there can have been relatively few forms of Christianity since then that have not merited the epithet 'Jewish' in this way, since a form of Christianity that did not merit it in this sense would be in large measure rootless, torn from the stock that bore it). Moreover, at the period with which we are concerned there can have been few Christian communities that did not include amongst their membership Christians who were Jews by birth, as well as non-Jews who had come to Christianity by way of a greater or lesser attachment to the Jewish communities of the Dispersion. Certainly, if Romans 16 is addressed to the church at Rome as was argued in the first chapter, then the Roman church included some Jews (cf. Rom 16.3 with Acts 18.2; Rom 16.7, 11).

(b) Paul and some, perhaps many, other like-minded Christians of his day were Jews; theirs too was a form of 'Jewish Christianity' (despite the tendency of some to classify Paul and his version of

Christianity as 'gentile Christianity'), and they were 'Jewish Christians'. Yet he and they were regarded by many of their contemporaries as having betrayed Judaism and their Jewish heritage and identity. That feeling, we saw, nearly cost Paul his life on his last visit to Jerusalem. Paul and his fellows stood for a form of Christianity that had, it was felt – and not without justice – surrendered the distinctive marks and privileges of Judaism, and had thrown open Israel's glorious heritage to all comers, seemingly unconditionally; for they had preached that non-Jews had a share in salvation and belonged to God's people even if they made no effort to conform to the way of life which God had, the Jews believed, laid down for the chosen people.

Do we, then, find any evidence of 'Judaizing Christianity' in the earliest church in Rome? One source suggests very clearly and definitely that this was indeed the earliest form of Christianity there: a commentary on the Pauline letters attributed to Ambrose of Milan, whose author has since the time of Erasmus been referred to by the name 'Ambrosiaster', tells us that

> It is established that there were Jews living in Rome in the times of the apostles, and that those Jews who had believed [in Christ] passed on to the Romans the tradition that they ought to profess Christ but keep the law (*ut Christum profitentes, legem servarent*) ... One ought not to condemn the Romans, but to praise their faith; because without seeing any signs or miracles and without seeing any of the apostles, they nevertheless accepted faith in Christ, although according to a Jewish rite (*ritu licet Judaico* – found only in Codex K). (In *CSEL* 81.1, 5-6; ET according to Donfried, *Debate* 54, following J. Knox in *IB* 9, 362.)

This work is thought to stem from Rome in the second half of the fourth century (so Altaner–Stuiber, *Patrologie* 389-90), and by itself would be perhaps a witness of uncertain character with regard to conditions obtaining in the Roman church so much earlier. Yet it is hard to think whence this picture of the Roman church might have arisen except through historical tradition.

At this point we need, however, to be clear that not all who professed this 'Judaizing' form of Christianity need have been

51

Jews by birth; many may well have been of gentile origin, but had espoused Judaism as proselytes, either before accepting a form of Christianity or, conceivably, at the time of receiving it in a form that embraced adherence to Judaism as part of its message (cf. Harder, 'Anlaß' 17). Schmithals goes further (*Römerbrief*, esp. 56-90): faced with the oft-noted paradox that the Roman Christians addressed were clearly gentiles, and yet that the argument of the first eleven chapters has its place in discussions with the synagogue (23), he argues that we have no choice but to postulate Judaizing gentile Christians as its readership; these are influenced by Judaism, hold Jewish views, and are preoccupied with Jewish problems (83; cf. also Suhl, 'Anlaß' 127).

Moreover we can perhaps see further evidence that would support the witness of 'Ambrosiaster'. For a start the Letter to the Hebrews, however mysterious its provenance and the identity of its author may be, can plausibly be regarded as sent to the church at Rome. At least that seems the most natural explanation for the closing greeting from 'those from Italy' (Heb 13.24): those who have come from Italy and are with the author of Hebrews wherever he or she is, join in sending their greetings back to the church to which this letter (if we may still call it a letter) is sent, and they would be most likely to do that if that church was the one from which they stemmed (cf. Brown–Meier, *Antioch* 146-9). But in that case we have here being sent to Italy, and most likely Rome, a writing that makes best sense if directed to Christians in danger of succumbing to the attractions of the Jewish cult, or perhaps returning to it; they therefore need to be shown the superiority of Christians' belief in the all-sufficiency of Christ's atoning work as it is interpreted on the analogy of the Jewish cult and shown both to surpass that cult and to fulfil all that it promised and foreshadowed. They are, moreover, warned not to neglect their meetings (*episynagōgē*, 10.25) as is the practice of some. This has caused some problems for interpreters, but many have suggested that in fact they are deserting their Christian meetings for Judaism. One could understand how that could very easily happen if those addressed had been accustomed before becoming Christians to worship in the Jewish synagogues and had still continued this association after becoming Christians; as Christians they might well also have had a further set of distinctively Christian gatherings (the preposition *epi* can mean 'in addition to'; is this the reason for the writer's choice of *episynagōgē* rather than plain *synagōgē* ?) .[4] If their sense of the distinctiveness of Christianity waned, it is easy to see how their motivation to double their attendance at religious meetings, both Jewish and Christian, would then also decline. Not all would have the time for that. But such a falling off in attendance at Christian meetings is not rebuked in such strong terms as we might expect if they were in danger of deserting Christianity for allegiance to some other deity or none. This warning of Hebrews makes best sense, then, directed to Christians who are strongly attracted to Judaism and Jewish ways of life and worship; their desertion of the Christian meetings would still mean that they continued to worship the same God, but now in only one way and no longer in two perhaps overlapping, but still different, communities. Hebrews, then, may be further evidence, however tentative, for a Judaizing form of Christianity in the Roman church, possibly at a somewhat later date than Paul's writing of Romans.[5]

The *First Letter of Clement* is firmer evidence in that we know that it was written from Rome, and in the last decade of the first century. It is striking that it describes the cultic service allotted to the Jewish high-priest, the priests and the Levites; the lay-person too 'is bound by the ordinances for the laity' (40.5, tr. Lake); sacrifices are offered only in Jerusalem (41.2 – the present tense is used despite the fact that the Temple was by now in ruins). There is no hint of criticism, no suggestion that the Jerusalem cult, quite apart from its fate at the hands of the Romans, had been superseded by the Christian one, and the Jewish ordinances are described in the present tense. It is true that Clement's point is to compare the divinely ordained Jewish cultic order with the similarly divinely authorized Christian order, but still the absence of any criticism of the Jewish cult remains. In the light of that it is perhaps also worth asking whether there is any significance that a few years later Ignatius of Antioch chooses to address his letter to the Roman church as 'to those who are united in flesh and spirit in every one of [God's] commandments' (tr. Lake).

In the end, however, evidence for the nature of the Christian traditions at Rome remains tantalizingly scanty. That they were originally of a Judaizing character must remain a hypothesis, nothing more. But this will be a hypothesis that gains in plausibility the better it helps to explain the character of Paul's letter to the Christians of Rome.

3. Claudius' Expulsion of the Jews

There is, however, one other possible piece of evidence. The Roman historian Suetonius, in his account of the life of the emperor Claudius, tells us that

> Since the Jews constantly made disturbances at the instiga-
> tion of Chrestus, he [Claudius] expelled them from Rome
> (25.4, tr. Rolfe).

Most see in the mention of 'Chrestus' a confused reference to 'Christus', Christ, and thus hold this to be evidence of distur-bances within the Jewish community at Rome caused by preach-ing about Christ. This is the more plausible in that Acts 18.2 tells us that Aquila and Priscilla had come to Corinth shortly before Paul's arrival there, having left Rome 'because Claudius had decreed that all Jews should leave Rome'; Paul's joining them becomes the more intelligible if they shared with him not only a common trade (Acts 18.3: 'tentmakers', i.e. leatherworkers according to Hock, *Context*), but also a common faith. Certainly Acts never mentions their conversion after their meeting Paul. If Christians had indeed been in large measure responsible for the disturbances amongst the Jewish community in Rome, then it is not surprising to find a Jewish Christian couple amongst the expelled Jews, for a Roman Jew who was also a Christian would be caught right in the midst of whatever storm of that sort blew up.

However, if most agree that 'Chrestus' is likely to be a reference to 'Christus', there the agreement ends. There is little agreement as to what sort of preaching of 'Christus' is likely to have caused the disturbances. There is, for instance, the suggestion of M. J. Borg

THE REASONS FOR ROMANS

that the 'Christus' involved in the disturbances was the Jewish
Messiah as proclaimed by Jewish nationalists and that the troubles
were therefore purely Jewish ones, caused by nationalistic fervour
and messianic expectations on the part of some of the Jewish
community in Rome: they looked for a God-given leader who
would free them from the Romans ('Context', esp. 212).
However, unless Jews were as a result expelled from Rome
regardless of whether they were implicated in this agitation or not
(and we saw earlier that it was unlikely that *all* Jews were involved
in view of their numbers), it is hard to explain why Aquila and
Prisca (or Priscilla as Acts calls her) were also expelled if indeed
they were Christians. And expulsion from Rome seems a surprisingly mild reaction to so overtly political a threat. Borg
appeals to Acts' silence about any connection between the
expulsion and Christian preaching, but this is hardly a persuasive
argument; for to mention this would run completely counter to
the apologetic concerns of this work, for it would then have to
admit that the Christian movement had been responsible for civil
disorder in Rome. Borg also appeals to Roman Jews' relative
ignorance of Christianity according to Acts 28.2; a footnote rather
undermines this argument, however, by conceding that a Jewish
community numbering, he suggests, perhaps 50,000 would not *all*
be likely to be familiar with a Christian community numbering
'perhaps a few hundred'; for it could equally well be argued that
not all Jews would have been immediately involved in confrontation with Christian preachers, but perhaps rather only one or two
of their numerous synagogues. Moreover Borg's argument perhaps places too great reliance on the strict historical accuracy of
Acts' presentation at this point; the writer cannot deny the
existence of Christians at Rome at this time, but he has not
explained how they got there or how the church was founded;
they are something of an anomaly in his account, and it may
therefore suit him to play down their importance and their
influence.

A more common source of disagreement at this point is over the
nature of the Christian preaching that caused the disturbances in
the Jewish community. For some it was simply the preaching of

Christ *per se*, and this could have been done by Judaizing Christians faithful to the Law. Yet would this alone have stirred up such strife? However, if Aquila and Prisca were involved, and if they were subsequently associated with Paul in his Corinthian ministry, then it is more likely that they at least were, like Paul, also representatives of a form of Christianity which held that non-Jews could become part of God's people without submitting to the Jewish Law. The same is perhaps also true of some of the other Jewish Christians whom Paul greets in Romans 16. Does that not suggest that the troubles in the Roman synagogues arose from causes rather similar to those which apparently provoked the hostility to Stephen in the Jerusalem synagogue for Diaspora Jews mentioned in Acts 6.9? That is to say that it was felt by the Roman Jews that Christians like Aquila and Prisca were also, like Stephen, 'saying blasphemous things against Moses and God' (cf. Acts 6.11) and against the Law (cf. 6.13), by proclaiming a Messiah who had changed the national way of life of the Jews (cf. 6.14, despite the future tense there).[6]

That is surely a more likely cause of strife than simply the preaching of Christ *per se* ; for Acts plausibly depicts such a preaching by Peter and his fellows in Jerusalem, when combined with faithfulness to the Temple and presumably also to the Law, as provoking opposition only from the Jewish leaders; that is understandable, for they would then have been implicated in the death of the one now proclaimed as God's Anointed. Such Christians apparently enjoyed popular respect and esteem, just as James the brother of Jesus and those with him seemingly did at a slightly later stage in the history of the Jerusalem church; it is only with the activities of Stephen and his fellow Hellenist Christians in Acts chap. 6 that the picture changes and popular resistance to the new faith arises. Few of the Roman Jews could have felt threatened by the mere preaching of Jesus as the promised Messiah or Christ in the same way as the Jewish leaders in Jerusalem were, whereas a message that seemed to undermine the distinctions between them and the surrounding pagan world in the name of this new Christ, and to subvert their national and communal identity, could have appeared very threatening to them.

If this explanation is correct, then Suetonius' account suggests that the situation which provoked the expulsion, probably in 49 C.E., was not a new one. Francis Watson rightly underlines the fact that Suetonius says that the Jews had 'constantly (*assidue*) made disturbances'; that implies more than one single incident. He goes on plausibly to suggest that this may help to explain the apparent discrepancy between the fifth century Christian writer, Orosius, and the earlier Roman historian, Dio Cassius, writing in the early third century; for the former reports on the alleged authority of Josephus that this expulsion by Claudius took place in the ninth year of that emperor's reign (i.e. from 25th Jan. 49-24th Jan. 50 C.E.), a date which would allow it to be placed in 49 C.E. and would harmonize well with Acts' mention of it in connection with Paul's first visit to Corinth; however, Dio Cassius mentions that in 41 Claudius disciplined the Jews, not by expulsion, but by a ban on their meetings (60.6.6). Gerd Lüdemann (*Paulus* 1, 183-95=ET 164-71) argues, despite Dio's explicit statement that the Jews were not expelled in 41, that this was in fact the true date of that expulsion; his case would have been stronger had that section of Dio's history survived that covers the year 49; since it has not, except in a brief summary that concentrates on other matters, we cannot say whether or not he was silent about any expulsion in that year. Watson plausibly concludes that it may be that

> disorders among the Roman Jews because of the preaching of the Christian gospel had been going on for some time before Claudius finally lost patience and expelled them in AD 49. His decree forbidding meetings of AD 41 may therefore have been an earlier measure designed to solve the same problem. This would suggest that the origins of Roman Christianity are to be placed at least as far back as the beginning of Claudius' reign (*Paul* 93).

Not only that, we may add, but, if the arguments above and the analysis of the probable causes of the disorders in the synagogues are correct, then already by that date that version of Christianity which would provoke such disturbances was already making its presence felt there; that means that the Pauline version of the gospel, offering a place in God's people to gentiles who did not observe the Jewish Law, was already known in Rome by then.

If all this reconstruction of events and of the earliest history of the Roman church is accepted, then this throws considerable light upon the situation in the Roman church at the time when Paul wrote to it. That church may originally have been, as 'Ambrosiaster' suggests, familiar only with a form of the Christian gospel which required all Christians to be faithful in their observance of the Jewish Law; yet the evidence and the arguments which we have just considered suggest that by little more than a decade at the latest after Jesus' death another version of the Christian gospel was making its presence felt in the capital city, a version which offered to non-Jews salvation and membership in God's people without requiring any observance of the Law and without compelling them to become Jews. We have seen that the reasons why this message should provoke resentment among Jews are not hard to find, and that it is likely that it is in the preaching of such a gospel that we should seek the cause of the troubles that led to Claudius' actions against the Roman Jewish community during the 40's.

If that is so then it is likely that, despite Acts 28.21, many of the Jews of Rome were indeed all too familiar with the form of the Christian message which Paul preached long before he arrived there as a prisoner around the year 60 C.E., and that they had good cause to suspect and resent that message as well as Paul himself who was its most conspicuous proponent.

However, it would be wrong to suppose that this is a feeling that would be confined to non-Christian Jews. If the Jews in the church in Jerusalem included many who were 'zealous for the Law' and who needed to be reassured lest Paul was encouraging Jews to desert their faith and the practice of circumcision (Acts 21.20-1), it is not unlikely that some Christian Jews at Rome shared a similar zeal for the Law and a similar suspicion of Paul. A number of scholars have, after all, posited close links and communications between Palestinian Jews and those at Rome, and similar ties may have existed between Christian Jews in both places.

In that case is it not misplaced to seek to distinguish, as some do (e.g. Schmithals, *Römerbrief*), between arguments in Romans that presuppose Jewish criticisms of Paul's gospel and ones which are appropriate to Jewish Christian criticisms of that message? For in large measure the grounds upon which Jewish Christians might criticize that gospel would be the same as those motivating non-Christian Jews: this was a message which called in question God's purposes with Israel and God's promises to the chosen people; it was a message that reduced Israel to the level of the surrounding nations, and called in question the value of the distinctiveness of its national way of life; this message removed the incentive to live differently to the surrounding nations, and thus threatened to plunge all into that morass of immorality which the Jews regarded as typical of the surrounding pagan culture. These were charges that both non-Christian Jews and Jewish Christians who upheld the continued necessity of the observance of the Law of Moses would level against a gospel that denied the necessity of that observance. They would also, indeed, be charges that would presumably also have seemed valid to such non-Jewish Christians as were were also persuaded of the necessity to keep the Jewish Law. It is, then, not so much the nature of the criticisms of Paul's gospel that reveals whether he had in mind the charges of non-Christian Jews or of Judaizing Christians, but rather the presuppositions upon which he bases his argument: did he appeal to assumptions that non-Christian Jews would share, or to ones with which only Jews who were, like himself, Christians would agree? To that question there can only be one answer, unless we suppose that Paul was very much arguing at cross-purposes in this letter: he assumes that God's final revelation has taken place in Christ and argues on that basis and from that presupposition. That argument would only carry weight with Christians.

4. The Evidence of Chapters 13-15

Already in chapter 2 §2 above it was suggested that Romans 14 reflects an actual situation in the Roman church, one where some held it necessary for Christians to observe the Jewish Law in matters of food and drink, and to observe certain days, and others considered such observances to be a symptom of a weakness in one's Christian faith: those whose faith was 'strong' were above such things and could ignore them. This is not, we also saw, quite the same as the division between Jewish Christians and gentile Christians, for there were undoubtedly Jewish Christians like Paul who shared the position of the 'strong in faith', and who had even preached to those strong that version of the Christian gospel upon which they based their claim to freedom from, and superiority to, the prescriptions of the Jewish Law; equally there may well have been gentile Christians, particularly if there were some who had already been attached in some way or other to the Jewish synagogues before their acceptance of the message of Christ, who still believed it to be necessary to observe the Jewish Law, either wholly or in part, and who were thus critical of Paul and those who followed him or agreed with him in his version of the Christian gospel.

There is, however, no mention in all this of the rite of circumcision. Seemingly that was not an issue at Rome, any more than it seems to have been in Corinth. (Where it is mentioned in 1 or 2 Corinthians it seems to be more as an illustration than as relating to an actual controversy in Corinth: 1 Cor 7.18-19.) In this Romans differs markedly from Galatians, for in the churches of Galatia this rite seems to have been the key issue. Whereas in Galatians Paul sums up his position by saying that God's new creation has superseded and replaced the distinction between circumcised and uncircumcised (6.15; cf. 3.28), in Romans God's reign is a matter of righteousness, peace and joy imparted by God's spirit, and this thus renders redundant questions concerning food and drink (14.17); the focus of the Judaizing controversy thus seems to have shifted from the question of circumcision and whether it is necessary for all Christians to the question of food and drink. 1 Cor 7.19 contains another such declaration, rather similar to that of Gal 6.15, but there circumcision and uncircumcision have been superseded, not by God's new creation, but by keeping God's commands – one can readily see why Paul would not want to make that contrast when confronted by the Judaizers'

THE REASONS FOR ROMANS

demand that his Galatian converts should keep the Jewish Law, but would feel it appropriate when the challenge confronting him in the Corinthian church included a strong libertine tendency, that is, a tendency to see Christianity as entitling one to do anything that the Jewish Law forbade. The way in which food and drink are superseded in Rom 14.17, rather than circumcision and uncircumcision, perhaps suggests the presence in Rome of a form of Judaizing Christianity which was more moderate in its demands upon non-Jewish Christians than Paul's opponents in Galatia were; the former may simply have required that gentile Christians keep a basic minimum of Jewish ritual requirements that would make fellowship between Jewish and non-Jewish Christians possible without compromising the former's faithfulness to Judaism. Whether this adherence to a limited range of Jewish enactments entitled the gentile Christians to an equal status in God's people alongside Jewish Christians, either in theory or in practice, is another matter; it should not be too quickly assumed that the former would enjoy equality if they simply kept these requirements. And even if in theory they were equal, that would not prevent them from being treated in practice as if they were fringe members, in much the same way as adherents to the synagogue who did not commit themselves to keep the Law of Moses in its entirety must have felt that they did not wholly belong to the Jewish community.

Another possible explanation of the absence of any mention of circumcision in chapter 14 is that it may be that for some Christians who were not Jews by birth, but had joined the Jewish community before they became Christians, perhaps even before they had heard of Christianity, the issue of circumcision was a thing of the past (cf. Suhl, 'Anlaß' 127); in joining the Jewish community they had already decided to submit to circumcision. Now with the preaching of a Law-free gospel the issue would be whether to continue with Jewish ritual requirements concerning food, drink and special days; there was no need to re-open the question of circumcision; they had decided on that before, and it was something that was easier to live with than to undo by undergoing a second, even more painful operation (cf. 1 Cor 7.18:

Paul counsels against anyone who was already circumcised on becoming a Christian seeking to reverse this operation). However it was still open to them either to persist in Jewish practices which were repeatable or to give them up, and so it may be that the argument in Rome was carried on with regard to matters of one's ongoing obedience to the Law of Moses, rather than with regard to this once and for all Jewish initiatory rite.

Thus, whatever explanation of the particular agenda for discussion and argument between Judaizing Christianity and supporters of a Law-free gospel at Rome is more likely, there seems to be good reason to suppose that these were actual issues in that community on which Paul offers advice; the issues and his approach to them differ sufficiently, as we have seen, from anything in either Galatians or 1 Corinthians to make it plausible to suggest that he is responding afresh to a new and in some significant respects different situation in the Roman church. That in turn suggests that he was sufficiently well informed about the Roman situation to accommodate his instructions to their actual situation.

There is one more piece of evidence that suggests a perhaps surprising awareness of that situation on Paul's part. In 1976 three German scholars, J. Friedrich, W. Pöhlmann and P. Stuhlmacher, published jointly an article on Rom 13.1-7 ('Situation'). In the course of that they suggested that the instructions about paying taxes in 13.6-7, which are unusual in literature of that period, either in Jewish material or in other literature of the Graeco-Roman world, are to be understood against the background of unrest in Rome at that time over the practices of those who collected the indirect taxes. In 58 C.E., Tacitus tells us (*Ann.* 13.50-1) there was such popular outcry against those responsible for the collection of indirect taxation that the emperor Nero was forced to intervene. He was persuaded by his advisers not to abolish such taxes outright, but the regulations governing their collection were to be published and enforced more rigorously to restrain the rapacity of the collectors. Suetonius simply tells us (*Nero* 10.1) that Nero abolished or mitigated the most grievous burdens of this sort of taxation.

It is certainly striking that Paul wrote these instructions, which we have said were somewhat unusual (Philo, for instance, betrays a far more negative attitude to tax-collectors: *Spec. leg.* 2.93-5; 3.159-63), at the very time when the agitation which eventually forced Nero to act must have been gathering strength; matters came to a head in 58, and Paul probably wrote Romans from Corinth in late 57 or early 58.

If that reconstruction is correct, then again it shows a surprisingly intimate knowledge by Paul, not only of the circumstances within the Roman church, but also of the situation in which its members had to live, and of the social, economic and political environment that surrounded them. It should be recalled, too, that the burden of these taxes or tolls would be felt particularly acutely by members of that social group who probably provided Paul's lines of communications with the Roman church, those who travelled for the purpose of trade. We can argue that Paul knew a great deal about what was going on in Rome, and that his advice to them was written in the light of that knowledge, and is to be interpreted by us in the light of that situation.

In investigating any of Paul's letters there is a large measure of reading between the lines involved in the reconstruction of the situation in which the recipients found themselves, for we always have to gauge that situation at second hand from what Paul says to his readers. They, however, do not need to be told all those things about their own situation which we need to know and want to discover; hence it is not surprising that the insights and clues which Paul offers us are never anything better than tantalizing hints about, and glimpses into, the circumstances in the church to which he was writing. Our efforts to assess those situations remain at best hypothetical, and it is small wonder that scholars differ from one another in their reconstructions (cf. in chap. 2 §2 above). The differences arise from the very nature of the evidence, and do not show that there is nothing to reconstruct or that Paul is addressing a hypothetical situation. There is a set of circumstances obtaining in each church to which he writes, even if it is largely hidden from the twentieth century critic. In this respect Romans is no different from any other letter which Paul wrote, or at least any difference, if there is one, is a matter of degree alone; moreover the degree of difference, if any, is but a small one.

The plausibility of any assessment of the likely situation in the church at Rome or in any church to which Paul wrote must be judged on the basis of at least three criteria:

(1) Is the situation presupposed inherently plausible? Does it provide a coherent picture of the life of the Christian community in that place?

(2) Is this picture compatible with what we know from other sources concerning the history of the earliest church? Is it similar to anything else we know happened elsewhere in the church of that day?

(3) Does it fit in with what Paul's text says? Does it make good sense of that text?

The more our proffered reconstructions square with these three criteria the more plausible they must be reckoned to be, but it will always remain a matter of greater or lesser plausibility, and nothing more.

One reconstruction which, it seems to me, makes good sense and responds well to the challenge of these three criteria is the one suggested above: the Roman church was *originally strongly Judaizing in character* , and the form of Christianity which was originally established in that city was one which combined belief in Christ with adherence to the Jewish Law. That version of Christianity may have been espoused by some gentiles as well as Jews, particularly by gentiles who had already been in contact with the Jewish synagogues. *Into that situation had come Christians proclaiming a different version of the Christian message, one which dispensed with the need for obedience to the Jewish Law as such*. This latter group gained in numbers and strength with the passage of time – it was, after all, far more attractive to non-Jews for whom keeping the Law was a considerable disincentive – whereas the strength of the Judaizing stream within the Roman church had been seriously weakened by Claudius' disciplinary measures against members of the Jewish community. Some protagonists of the Law-free Christian gospel, such as

Aquila and Prisca, are likely to have been affected too, but it was to be expected that these measures would bear disproportionately severely upon that part of the Roman church which contained more Jewish members. By the time that Paul wrote, however, Claudius was dead, and his edict of expulsion, if it had not been repealed, may at least have lapsed, so that Jews could freely move back into Rome (see the arguments of Wiefel mentioned in chap. 1 §2); it was also to be expected that the strength of the Judaizing tradition in the church there would be increased again, as well as the non-Christian Jewish community in the capital city, bringing with it the risk of further troubles in the form of friction between proponents of the Law-free gospel and their Jewish and Judaizing neighbours. Part of that danger, the risk of friction between Judaizing Christians and supporters of a Law-free gospel, Paul seeks to avert by appealing for mutual tolerance and esteem. Such a scenario makes a great deal of sense of part of the contents of Romans, but only of a part, and it is the argument of this study that a satisfactory account of 'the reasons for Romans' will have to make sense of the whole letter.

IV

THE INTERRELATION OF PAUL'S CIRCUMSTANCES AND THE ROMAN CHURCH'S

The demand for a coherent account of the circumstances in the Roman church which could explain both Paul's writing of Romans and the contents of the letter as a whole forces us to try to bring together the letter's evidence for Paul's own situation when writing it (chapter 2) as well as the possible indications which we have just seen (in chapter 3) of the situation in the Roman church, and also too to combine with these two an explanation of those parts of Romans whose presence and nature has not yet been adequately explained. These unexplained parts include, disconcertingly, the bulk of the argument of the letter which is found in chapters 1-11 as well as the seemingly more general advice offered by Paul to the Romans in chapter 12.

In trying to do this we will often find ourselves reading more into the text of Romans than actually lies upon the surface of the text, and may often seem to extract more from the text than it actually seems to say. In case this seems to be an illegitimate or arbitrary way of proceeding it may be said in its defence that often one has to read between the lines of texts in order to make sense of what they say; rarely does a writer set down absolutely everything that is necessary for the understanding of his or her ideas and of the connections between them. If that is true of the writer of a monograph or treatise, and undoubtedly it is true of this all too brief study, then how much more will it be true of the author of a letter, dictating it to an amanuensis as was the case with Romans (16.22)? It would not be surprising if Paul's thoughts galloped ahead of what Tertius could get down in writing, nor if the limits of the time available and of ancient writing materials curbed Paul from saying much of what he could have said in exposition of such complex ideas and such profound themes. And yet there must be some control over what one reads between the lines. If there is any then it must be that, firstly, what is read between the lines must not contradict what is palpably set forth in the lines, and, secondly, it will become the more plausible the better it helps to explain the connections between the ideas actually expressed in the text. A limitation is, however, placed on the validity of these criteria by our uncertainty as to how accurately the text expressed what Paul actually meant to say and also as to how well connected his ideas actually were. Yet, other things being equal, he can perhaps be given the benefit of the doubt, and the logicality and orderliness and consistency of his thought at a given point can perhaps be assumed until we see good reason to call it into question.

As we try to discern the relation between the situations of Paul and the Roman Christians on the one hand and the contents of chapters 1-12 on the other, it is in fact with the opening words of chapter 12 that we can perhaps most conveniently approach this problem, as we try to evaluate the claims made for the function and significance of the particular form of words which Paul uses to introduce this hortatory part of his letter to the Romans.

1. *Parakalō*

Carl J. Bjerkelund dedicated a monograph to the study of sentences introduced by the word *parakalō*, 'I beg, urge', in Paul's letters. These sentences typically are introduced by this verb in the first person singular (or plural), followed by a conjunction (*oun* or *de*) and the object, the second person pronoun *hymas*, 'you', often with the vocative *adelphoi* ; in a number of cases a prepositional phrase then follows, *dia* with a genitive, and then the actual request, expressed either by an infinitival construction or by an imperative or by a clause introduced by the conjunction *hina*. These formal observations are the more significant in that Romans contains three examples of this construction:[1]

12.1-2: So (*oun*) I beg (*parakalō*) you (*hymas*), brothers (*adelphoi*) by (*dia*) God's mercies to offer (infinitive) ... Do not be conformed (imperative) ..., but be transformed (imperative) ... .

15.30: ['But' (*de*) is omitted in many modern translations] I urge (*parakalō*) you (*hymas*), ['brothers' (*adelphoi*): only found in some MSS and omitted by some important ones], by (*dia*) our Lord Jesus Christ and by (*dia*) the love that the Spirit gives, to struggle (infinitive) ... [the following *hina*-clauses do not contain the content of his request, but rather the purpose of their struggling in prayer].

16.17:['But' (*de*) is again usually omitted] I urge (*parakalō*) you (*hymas*), brothers (*adelphoi*), to watch out (infinitive) ... and avoid (imperative) ... .

Most features of this construction can readily be paralleled in other extant letters from antiquity, although it is hard to find examples of the prepositional phrases used above. It is a form of request used among friends; it also finds its place in official communications between friends and equals, and in the speeches related by a historian like Polybius (second century B.C.E.) it is, for instance, used by envoys to make their requests; the Jewish historian Josephus also sometimes uses it in diplomatic letters and speeches which he cites in his *Jewish Antiquities* as well as once in a farewell speech.[2] That fact deserves all the more attention in view of Robert Jewett's likening Romans to an 'ambassadorial letter' (see chap. 1 §1 above) and in view of the fact that Paul was writing to the Roman church in such a way as to avoid seeming to impose his authority upon them. Conversely the absence of this verb or this construction (apart from one example of what Bjerkelund recognizes as a kindred construction) from Galatians may be symptomatic of the way in which Paul's relations with that church may have degenerated so far that he dispensed with diplomatic niceties.

The appropriateness of this form of words in diplomatic usage becomes clearer still when Bjerkelund turns to Paul's use of it. For in Philemon 8 and 9 it becomes plain from Paul's contrast of commanding (*epitassō*) and requesting that this is a form appropriate for requests made to an equal whose relation to the one making the request is characterized by love (cf. vv 7 and 8). This same letter also shows how a variant form of this construction is used to introduce Paul's chief point in writing the letter (vv 9-12).

In Romans another typical feature of Paul's letters which corresponds to ancient epistolary practice also appears: a thanksgiving (1.8ff) is followed by an appeal introduced by *parakalō* (15.30ff); moreover the subject matter of the thanksgiving is often directly connected to that of the request, in that the former somehow paves the way for the latter. However here these two elements are far more widely separated from one another than elsewhere. Yet this should not blind us, Bjerkelund argues, to the integral connection between the two, the thanksgiving emphasizing Paul's desire to visit Rome, which is also mentioned again in 15.22-4, and his request to the Roman church to strive with him in prayer for the success of his planned visit to Jerusalem with the collection. We might say that 15.22-4 serves the purpose of restoring the connection between the subject matter of the thanksgiving and the request of 15.30-2, a connection that might otherwise be lost from sight through the extent of the intervening material. Bjerkelund argues that the request of 15.30ff must be considered as of considerable importance within the letter, yet his arguments for this are not wholly convincing: (1) he argues that the request of 15.30ff echoes the introductory thanksgiving, and that this shows the store that Paul set by his planned trip to Rome. Yet the thanksgiving concerns a journey to Rome and the request a journey to Jerusalem, and Bjerkelund nowhere shows how these journeys are connected. (2) He points out too that the twofold requests of 12.1-2 and 15.30-2 are unusual in Paul's letters in that both contain prepositional phrases; normally, where more than one request with *parakalō* occurs in a letter, only the first is reinforced by such a phrase. This is an interesting observation, but in itself it is not enough to justify Bjerkelund's conclusion that 'one may rightly ask whether the *parakalō*-sentence in 15.30ff does not express the true purpose that Paul seeks to achieve in Romans' (158). (And he is not alone in this opinion: Jervell, 'Letter' 66, comments, 'The reason for writing Romans is expressed in 15:30-32'.) If this were true (and the title of this study, it will be recalled, deliberately uses the plural 'reasons' to safeguard against the assumption that there is simply one reason why Paul wrote Romans), then the case would have to be made with greater rigour of argument. For a start one might rather expect the occurrence of two appeals introduced by *parakalō* reinforced by prepositional phrases to mean that Paul rather had two true purposes in writing Romans and not just one. That in turn would also invite the question what was the relation between these two requests, and what was the relation between the first of them, 12.1-2, and the thanksgiving; why should the relationship only exist between the thanksgiving and the second example of this construction in the letter?

Bjerkelund's arguments provide a useful starting point, however, for this chapter in that he brings together Paul's thanksgiving in 1.8ff and his request in 15.30-2. The former introduces something that Paul will do which directly affects the Roman Christians: he is planning to visit them. The latter deals with something which apparently does not affect them: he is planning to visit the church at Jerusalem bringing them the collection. Yet Paul does ask them to do something about this visit: they are asked to support it in prayer. Is his visit to Jerusalem then a more direct concern of theirs than might at first sight seem to be the case? And is there in fact any relationship between this visit to Jerusalem and the planned subsequent visit to Rome? This will be the subject matter of §2 below.

The gaps in Bjerkelund's arguments also raised another question that is relevant here: if the thanksgiving ought to be related to Paul's request in 12.1-2 as well as to that in 15.30-2, what might that relationship be? In other words, what possible bearing might the exhortations and advice offered in 12.1-2, and perhaps in the following chapters as well which are introduced by this appeal, have upon his proposed visit to Rome? To this we shall turn in §3.

2. The Roman Christians' Relationship to the Collection

In looking at the question of the collection in chapter 2 §3 we saw how controversial a project this would have been in the eyes of the

Jerusalem Christians, and how they might well have felt that to accept the proffered gift was not worth the risk. For to accept it would seem to be an endorsement of Paul's mission and an expression of solidarity with his churches; that would seem to Jewish Christians who were zealous for the Law and jealously preserved their ancestral heritage to be a betrayal of their traditions and a repudiation of their identity as the true and faithful remnant of Israel,[3] as well as endangering them in the eyes of their fellow Jews by making them seem to be traitors to their nation.

One can therefore see why Paul might ask for prayer for this venture, prayer that his gift might be accepted, for there was a very real danger that it might not be. Yet, despite Bjerkelund's suggestion that this request for prayer for Paul's safety and for the acceptability of the collection is the true purpose of Paul's writing Romans, it is hard to see how this can be the key to the purpose of the letter. For Paul does little to explain to the Roman church the reasons for, and the rationale of, the collection, and as it stands Bjerkelund's account seems to do little to show why the extensive and far-ranging doctrinal contents of the earlier parts of the letter were ever included if the explanation of the reasons for Romans stops at this point.

Yet there is perhaps, nevertheless, more to be said for Bjerkelund's proposal than meets the eye. That becomes clearer when we stop to ask *how the Roman Christians were connected with the collection.*For the Roman Christians too were amongst the gentiles or non-Jewish nations (1.5-6), who had shared in the spiritual gifts or riches of the Jerusalem Christians, and were therefore in duty bound to minister to the latter's needs in material things (15.27). It is true that Paul nevertheless does not ask them for contributions, but there are possibly at least two good reasons for that:

(1) The Roman Christians are not one of his churches, not one of his apostolic foundations, however much he may feel that they in fact come under his jurisdiction; he has to tread a diplomatic tightrope in writing to them at all, neither denying his God-given authority and responsibility which extends to them nor provoking

rejection by too blatant an exercise or imposition of his authority (cf. chap. 2 §1). He cannot therefore risk issuing instructions to them; they might not be willing to obey him, as we shall see.

(2) Anyway, to seek to involve the Roman church materially in the gathering of the collection at this late stage would involve a considerable delay, and would greatly complicate and drag out the preparations for this project, and Paul was a man in a hurry, filled with a restless energy to proclaim the message of Christ throughout the gentile world.

Thus it is intelligible that Paul does not ask for material contributions, but simply for their support in prayer. That would not delay his plans for the collection, now far advanced, nor did it run the same risk of provoking a refusal to help by the Roman Christians. But at least, as Wilckens puts it ('Abfassungszweck' 128), they should be there amongst the gentile Christians of the East in Jerusalem – at least in prayer.

For it needs to be recognized that Paul could not count upon the Roman Christians' wholehearted support for this project. If it is correct, as was argued in the previous chapter, that there were those in the Roman church who remained steadfastly loyal to the Jewish Law as well as those who espoused a form of Christianity which dispensed with the Law, then it follows that Paul's appeal for support in the collection venture would be likely to meet with a very varied response on the part of different members of the Roman church, and many of those responses would have probably been unfavourable.

Those loyal to the Jewish Law doubtless would have felt much the same about both Paul and the collection as did the Jerusalem church: they would have been reluctant to support the collection if their support seemed to confer respectability and the appearance of their approval and endorsement on a form of Christianity which they perhaps deplored and at least regarded with considerable suspicion. They were not in as great physical danger as their fellow Christians in Jerusalem, it is true, since they were not surrounded by a mass of non-Christian Jews, many of them strongly nationalistic and thus highly sensitive towards anything which they felt violated Jewish distinctiveness and privileges; yet

THE REASONS FOR ROMANS

perhaps even in Rome they might be at some risk too, if disorders arose once more within the Jewish synagogues of that city, provoked by the preaching of the Christian gospel in a form offensive to Jewish ears. But what they chiefly had in common with the Jerusalem Christians was a fierce loyalty to Judaism and their Jewish heritage, and this, they would have felt, was being cast aside by Paul and his gentile mission. Those that felt thus in the Roman church might well have hoped that, like themselves, the Jerusalem Christians would reject both Paul and his message and his churches full of ritually impure and immoral gentiles who had the audacity to claim that they were fully fellow-heirs with them to the spiritual inheritance of Israel; they would thus hope, too, that the Jerusalem church would reject the collection, and thus destroy the dangerous pretensions of these upstarts, by denying that they belonged together within the one true people of God.

On the other hand it might be thought that at least Paul could count on the support of those who, like him, espoused a Law-free gospel. But was this is in fact so? It must be remembered that there were followers of Paul in his churches who took the freedom from the Law preached by the apostle further than he himself wished or thought appropriate; that, at least, seems the most plausible explanation of the excesses of some at Corinth, seemingly under the slogan 'All is lawful' (1 Cor 6.12; 10.23), against which Paul had to contend in 1 Corinthians: they seem to have argued that their freedom from the Law extended to freedom from the Law's teaching against sexual immorality and idolatry. Such Christians are unlikely to have had much sympathy with anything that seemed to reinforce Christianity's ties with Judaism. The bringing of the collection to Jerusalem could all too easily seem like a Christian counterpart to the didrachma or half-shekel Temple-tax which Jews throughout the Diaspora used to send annually to Jerusalem up until the Jewish war and the sack of Jerusalem and the Temple by Titus in 70 C.E.[4] That impression could only be increased by Paul's referring to the collection as something 'owed' by gentile Christians to the Jerusalem church, despite the fact that individuals seemingly did not have to pay any fixed amount (1 Cor 16.2). Such a payment could seem to imply that the gentile

Christians were somehow tribute-paying vassals of the Jerusalem church and therefore also answerable to them and subject to their Judaizing version of the gospel. In Beker's words, it symbolized 'the salvation-historical priority of Israel and Jewish Christianity over the Gentiles' (*Paul* 72). However, the latter part of Romans 11 and in particular the image of the olive-tree there (11.17-24) suggest that there were some in the church at Rome who were not mindful of their spiritual debt to Israel, and held that Israel had been cast aside by God in order to make way for them, the gentiles (cf. esp. 11.19). In chapter 11 Paul must therefore remind his readers that these seemingly outcast Jews were nevertheless the true and original branches of God's olive tree, and in chapter 15 he must recall to them that they had been privileged to share in the spiritual riches of the Jerusalem church; the one reminder called them to a proper humility and gratitude towards the stock on to which they have been granted, the nation of Israel in general, the other to a sharing of their material resources with those of Israel who had let them share in their spiritual heritage, their materially less fortunate brothers and sisters in Christ in the Jerusalem church; for from that church the gospel had spread out to the gentile world and to them.

In short, *the Roman Christians were caught up in the collection by virtue of the facts that they were a gentile church, and that the collection was offered on behalf of the gentile churches, but it was by no means certain that all of them would welcome this involvement; for some it would seem to entail support of a movement within the church to which they were opposed and of which they were critical; to others it would seem to suggest dependence on, even subordination to, a church and a centre with which they felt they had few ties and towards which they felt little loyalty or reason for gratitude.* The appeal for support and intercession on behalf of the collection was thus one which brought to a head a number of issues that Paul's mission raised: the status of Israel and the Jewish Law, and the relation of both to the increasingly non-Jewish church which was emerging. The argument of this section has been that the Roman Christians were initially disposed to respond to such an appeal in two different ways and for two different sets of reasons, depending on whether they leaned more towards a Judaizing version of Christianity or one that sat loose to the Law and to Christianity's ties with Judaism. How was Paul to persuade both these groups differently, for otherwise he could not count on their support in his bringing of the collection to Jerusalem?

However Bjerkelund's study, as we saw, posed another problem, the relation of 12.1-2 to the collection and to Paul's subsequent visit to Rome, and to that question we must now first turn.

3. Romans 12.1ff and Paul's Visit to Rome

In §1 above it was pointed out that it was inconsistent of Bjerkelund to suggest that Rom 15.30-2 disclosed *the* true purpose of Romans when the same construction, upon which he based his argument, was also to be found in 12.1-2. It was, however, understandable that he should experience some difficulty in explaining why this seemingly very general exhortation should indicate another 'true purpose' of Paul's in writing Romans; seemingly Paul could have written something so general to any church at any time; it hardly explains why Paul wrote thus to this church at this time. The connection, too, between this exhortation and Paul's visit to Rome, which was the main theme of the thanksgiving of 1.8ff, which in turn should set the scene for the request which is the real point of the letter, is far from self-evident.

However Bjerkelund does perhaps also supply a clue that might help us to resolve this dilemma. He notes (*Parakalô* 161) that the appeal of 12.1, 'by God's mercies', provides a link with the immediately preceding passage, even if the theme of God's mercy is there expressed in terms of a different word to the one used here (*oiktirmos* ; in 11.30-2 the verb *eleeō* is used; however the cognate verb *oikteirō* was used earlier in 9.15 in a quotation of Exod 33.19 which uses these two verbs as parallels and synonyms). But he also suggests (ibid. 171) that the real emphasis in Paul's appeal is to be found at the end of v 2: they are to be renewed in their minds, 'in order to discern what God's will is, that which is good and pleasing (to God)[5] and perfect'. To anticipate the subsequent argument, I would suggest that, if it can be shown that these two verses not only link the following exhortations on to what has gone before (see further §4 below), but also announce a theme that is sustained throughout the following chapters, if they are, as it were, a heading for what follows, then it can be legitimately claimed that the construction upon which Bjerkelund based his study does indeed signal the true purpose of Romans, even if that purpose is in fact to be divided into a number of interrelated sub-objectives, one of which is announced later in 15.30-2.

The suggestion that these words at the end of 12.1-2 do indeed provide such a heading for what follows needs, however, to be supported by a great deal more argument than Bjerkelund provides. The exhortation to renewal of one's mind in v 2, it is to be noted, is followed immediately by a section dealing with how such a renewed mind should think (*phronein*, v 3): it starts with an exhortation that no one should hold an immoderately high estimate (*hyperphronein*) of themselves, but rather a moderate one (*sōphronein*) and this is echoed in 12.16, in a sort of 'ring-composition', that is by the argument, as it were, completing a full circle by returning to the same theme with which it began, by the appeal not to be haughty in one's thinking (*phronountes*) or to be 'wise' (*phronimoi*) in one's own eyes (cf. 11.25; the echo of this phrase again here underlines again the connection between these two parts of Romans), but to associate with the lowly.[6] The command in 12.17 to 'render' (*apodidontes*) evil to no one in return for evil then introduces another section dealing with Christians' response to evil, or what seems evil, offered to them by others, which is rounded off in 13.7 with another command to 'render' (*apodote*) to all what is 'due' to them, again a sort of ring-composition. The theme of the Christian's way of thinking is continued within this section by the command in 12.17*b* to set one's mind (*pronooumenoi*) on what is good in the sight of all people. 13.8-10 then picks up the idea of what is 'due' to others from 13.7 and concludes this section with the summary that to love is to fulfil the Law. The connection with 12.2 would have been plainer here had Paul said in so many words that to love was to do the will of God, but the sense is the same. We shall see below that there is probably a very good reason for Paul's rather unexpectedly introducing a reference to the Law here: it reinforces his earlier argument in which he sought to convince Jewish Christian critics of his gospel that that gospel does not involve the abandonment of the abiding will of God which is contained in that Law; in particular obedience to his gospel is not the unbridled descent into godless immorality which they alleged it to be. 13.11-14 then returns to the theme of the renewal of the Christian in a form befitting the new age: this renewal is now more vividly and concretely expressed in terms of a putting on of Christ, representing the humanity of that new age (v 14), but it is again a renewal affecting also one's way of thinking, for one is to make no provision (*pronoian* ; cf. 12.17*b*) for the flesh, that is, not to set one's mind on satisfying the needs and demands of the flesh.

With 14.1-15.13 the theme of one's way of thinking or set of mind, introduced in 12.2-3, is picked up once more. That is indicated by the appearance again here of the term *phronein* : 'the one who sets his mind (*phronōn*) on a particular day has this way of thinking (*phronei*) for the sake of the Lord' (14.6*a*); Paul prays that God may grant them a common mind (*phronein*) in 15.5. Again, doing what is pleasing to God (12.2) is, by implication, a dominant theme of 15.1ff: the 'strong' are not to please themselves (15.1) but their neighbour (15.2), just as Christ did not please himself (15.3). Implicit here is that Christ instead pleased God and that the person who pleases his neighbour pleases God too. The discerning (*dokimazein*) of God's will mentioned in 12.2 is picked up again at the conclusion of the argument of chapter 14 by the pronouncement in 14.22 that all are blessed who do not judge themselves (i.e. judge themselves unfavourably, or bring an unfavourable judgment upon themselves) in what they approve or discern (*dokimazei*) as the right course of action for themselves.

The upshot of this argument is to conclude that, *when Paul speaks in such seemingly general terms in 12.2 of the renewal of the Romans' minds, he already has in view a quite concrete application of this renewal: he wants them to view their fellow Christians in the Roman church in a new light, in the light of the new age in which they live and in the light of Christ, the representative person of that new age whom they must, as it were, put on. They must above all be able to discern God's will in the matter of their attitude to the ritual observances which are at issue between them, to see how they are concretely to serve God in a manner pleasing to God.*

It can also be argued that the rest of the contents of chapters 12 and 13 are far from being as general as many scholars suppose. (Even if individual pieces amongst their contents were found to be in large measure traditional, that would still not account for Paul's use of precisely these particular pieces of tradition chosen out from amongst all the mass of traditional ethical material that lay to hand in early Christianity and Greek-speaking Judaism.) We have already seen (in chapter 3 §4) how concrete and specific the commands of 13.6-7 may be, but the same applies more widely within these chapters: there we can see *a whole series of seemingly general instructions which take on a new immediacy when set in the context of the situation of the Roman church when they are read in the light of what follows, particularly in chapter 14, but also in chapter 15:*

(1) The warning against too high a self-estimate in **12.3** has a particular relevance to 'strong' Christians inclined to despise and disparage their fellow Christians who held to various Jewish ritual observances (cf. Dahl, 'Theology' 86, who links this verse and v 16 with 11.20). Significantly they are to form a modest estimate of themselves, 'as God has apportioned to each a measure of faith'. The reference to a 'measure of faith' is puzzling, but can be most readily understood against the background of a controversy over the relative 'strength' or 'weakness' of one's faith, measured by the degree to which one thinks Jewish legal observances are necessary for one's service of Christ.

(2) The remarks about the unity of Christians in the one 'body of Christ' with its many limbs in **12.4-5** arguably have as much relevance to a Roman church rent by quarrels over the observance of the Jewish Law as they had to a Corinthian church divided over the question of spiritual gifts and over the significance of the possession or non-possession of the more spectacular gifts.

However Paul does also go on in Rom **12.6-8** to discuss the diversity of gifts distributed to these different limbs in Christ's body. At first sight that is a development of the image of a body and its many limbs which was more relevant to the Corinthian situation than to the Roman church's. Yet the gifts that are mentioned in Romans are from being the same as those mentioned in 1 Corinthians where gifts like those of wisdom (12.8), knowledge (12.8; 13.2), faith in the sense of wonder-working faith (12.9; cf. 12.10, 28; 13.2) or healing (12.9, 28, 30), and above all speaking in tongues (12.10, 28, 30; chap. 14) were at the centre of controversy. *The examples in Romans are by no means a mere extrapolation from 1 Corinthians.*

'Prophecy' (Rom 12.6) is, it is true, one gift that is mentioned in 1 Corinthians, but here there is the puzzling addition that it should be exercised 'according to the proportion (*analogian*) of (the) faith'. Although the word *analogia*, 'proportion', is a different one it is hard not to connect this with the reference to the 'measure (*metron*) of faith' (with no definite article, but this may not be of any significance) two verses earlier. That prophecy should be mentioned is perhaps the more appropriate here in that the purpose of this gift was above all to make known God's will (cf. v 2); chapter 14 reflects a situation in which two sides set out their own views of God's will and the one accused the other of deficiencies in their faith. It is fitting in this situation that Paul should tell any who declared God's will to do so 'in proportion to their faith'. In all this he sides with the 'strong in faith', but seeks to deal even-handedly with both strong and weak; the weak too may declare God's will, it is surely implied, but their declarations should arise out of faith (cf. 14.23).

In the following verse 'teaching' is also mentioned, and this too has surely something to do with communicating a knowledge of God's will. However, whereas the prophet or prophetess laid claim to some more direct revelation from God, the teacher's function, we may surmise, although it too was concerned with communicating the will of God, lay more in the exposition of scripture and tradition. If that is the case it would follow that the teachers in the Roman church would be caught right in the maelstrom of the disputes there over the keeping or not keeping of the Jewish Law. In their exposition of the Old Testament and Christian tradition which tradition were they to say that one should follow – that which held that all parts of the Old Testament were binding on Christians and were still normative for their lives, or that propagated by those who, like Paul, held some of it (or all of it, one might suppose from some of Paul's utterances) to be superseded by the coming of Christ? Moreover, if the gift of 'exhortation' which is mentioned next in 12.8 is indeed closely linked to the task of teaching, then it too would be involved in the same responsibility of practical guidance amidst this particular cluster of problems affecting the life of the Roman church.

A further gift mentioned in 12.7 is that of 'service' (*diakonia*), a term that not only echoes Paul's description of his own ministry in 11.13, but also looks forward to chapter 15 where Paul will twice describe the collection to be offered to the Jerusalem church using this word and its cognate verb: he is going to Jerusalem in the service (*diakonōn*) of the saints (15.25), and he prays that his service (*diakonia*) may be acceptable to them (15.31). It may well be significant, therefore, that he also describes Christ as a 'servant (*diakonos*) of the circumcision' in 15.8: Paul's own actions towards the Jerusalem church echo those of his Lord, just as he had just previously argued that all Christians should imitate Christ in refraining from pleasing themselves (15.2-3). Although the Romans cannot contribute materially to this 'service', as we have seen, yet they are asked in 15.30-2 to involve themselves in it by praying for it, by standing by Paul in his service. In the light of this it is perhaps not far-fetched to suggest that the appeal in 12.8 to the one who gives a share in something to do so generously may also be written with an eye to the same project, even if the Romans are not actually involved in contributing financially themselves. The following advice may be to the Christian leader (*pro-istamenos*), but the position of the mention of this gift between mention of the gifts of sharing and of performing acts of mercy suggests that the alternative translation of this verb as referring to one who gives aid is to be preferred.

The reference in 12.8 to performing acts of mercy with gladness may also belong to this same context of the Romans' involvement in the collection project; but it is also another term which echoes the language of chapter 11, in this case, however, language there used to describe God (11.30-2; cf. 9.15-18, 23); the merciful action of God is also one which is mentioned again in 15.9. Paul's appeal to the Roman Christians gladly to exercise mercy would also therefore be particularly appropriate in writing to a church which so needed to be reminded of the mysterious but wonderful ways of a God whose ultimate purpose was to have mercy on all, both Jews and gentiles (11.32); this, too, was a church which Paul had reminded that they all alike depended for their hope upon God's mercy and grace. Judaizing Christians needed to be reminded that God's dealing with them was on the basis of mercy, but gentile Christians too, who were disposed to reject everything Jewish, needed to be reminded that they, like God, needed to deal mercifully with Jews and Jewish Christians, both in Rome and in Jerusalem.

It may seem that some of these comments on these various gifts which Paul mentions here press more out of Paul's exhortations than is warranted. On the other hand *we do need to explain why Paul chooses quite this particular list of gifts; it is, as far as we can see, far from being either comprehensive or standardized.* There are therefore considerable advantages in any interpretation that shows the more or less direct relevance of these instructions to the present situation of either Paul or the Roman church or both of these, and they do seem to have considerable relevance to a church split over the question of adherence to the Jewish Law and confronted with the question of support for the collection which raised all too acutely the issue of the validity of the Law-free gospel.

(3) The relevance of the exhortations which follow in **12.9-16** to a church split over these issues is far more immediately evident. For here Paul urges love (12.9), in particular love of one's fellow Christians (12.10) and mutual respect (12.10; cf. 12.16); they are to show this love in their sharing of each others' joy and grief (12.15). But the injunction to contribute (*koinōnountes*) to the needs of the

saints is, we have seen (chap. 2 §3), very similar to the language which Paul uses of the collection for the Jerusalem church, so similar in fact that it is hard to believe that Paul intended no reference to the collection here; there is therefore a strong case here for seeing Paul as looking again beyond the obligation to show love within the local congregation to the wider horizon of the Roman Christians' obligations to show a like concern for their brothers and sisters in the needy mother-church in Jerusalem. They are also to practise hospitality towards strangers, and that might also be an area of Christian obligations where mutual suspicion towards representatives of differing Christian traditions might have made Roman Christians less ready than they should have been to welcome any Christians who came to visit them.

We have already seen, too, that the closing appeal of this section echoes 12.3, but in other respects the passage anticipates later concerns of this part of Romans. The service (*douleuontes*, 12.11) of the Lord is a theme that runs through the first part of chapter 14 with its stress on the responsibility of each servant (*oiketēs*) of Christ to his or her master, be that master Christ or God (e.g. 14.4, 6, 8, 12). In the same chapter too, it will be recalled, Paul stresses the priority of 'righteousness, peace and joy in the holy spirit' (14.17) over questions of food and drink. Here in chapter 12 they are urged to yield to the leading of that same spirit.

(4) This section also includes, however, a command to bless, rather than curse, those who persecuted them (12.14). That anticipates the theme of the following section, **12.17-21**, which deals with Christians' response to ill-treatment at the hands of non-Christians. That treatment could come from non-Christian Jews, as 1 Thess 2.14-16 shows, and this actual fact of such persecution could only have encouraged many gentile Christians to write Israel off as accursed and rejected by God, as well as wishing them to be so accursed. The command to overcome evil with good (12.21) would then find a concrete illustration in the collection, which, even if it did not benefit Jews in general, but only the Jerusalem church, yet in so doing benefited a church which as a whole sided with unbelieving Jews in obstructing the

mission to the gentiles (cf. 1 Thess 2.16), at least on the terms that Paul carried it out.

(5) However, the next section, **13.1-7**, seems to deal with relationships of a very different sort, those between Christians and the civil authorities, and in particular with the Roman government if the very concrete reference of 13.6-7 argued for above at the end of the previous chapter is correct. Yet the preceding section had included the quite general commands to set their minds on aims that were good before all people and to live at peace as far as possible with all (12.17-18); that 'all' would also include the Roman authorities, and so this shift of subject was to that extent anticipated earlier. Yet it should be recalled that the Roman Christians might well have had cause to regard the Roman authorities as an oppressive power when they intervened in disturbances in the synagogue, and Jewish Christians of differing beliefs might well have regarded them as persecuting them when they drove them from Rome. (It was suggested earlier that these disturbances had been due to the antipathy of Jews and Judaizing Christians towards Christian preachers who proclaimed that God's offer of salvation to the gentiles did not entail the latter in keeping the Jewish Law, and the subsequent expulsion may have involved both Jewish Christians who resisted this version of the gospel and those who propagated it.) The question of taxes which may now have been a prime threat to the Roman Christians' relationship with the Roman government was not related to this issue at all, as far as we know, but it should rather perhaps be regarded as a potential cause of trouble *in addition to* the threat of renewed friction between Jews and Christians over the Law-free gospel, rather than as replacing that friction as the sole potential cause of the Roman rulers' wrath; for the potential for further strife over the claims of Christians about the admission of gentiles to God's people remained, and indeed was perhaps increasing if the Jewish population of Rome, both Christian and non-Christian, was growing in number again after the death of Claudius.

(6) **13.8-10** is linked to 12.9ff by the theme of love. Interestingly, and rather surprisingly, it is here linked to the keeping of the Jewish Law. That does make sense, however, within a context

where one group of Christians is very much concerned with obedience to the Law of Moses and is criticized by another group for that concern and in turn hold it against their critics that they do not keep the Law; that is the situation which it was suggested lay behind chapter 14, and it is a situation in which the relationships of the two groups could all too easily become unloving. There is therefore considerable significance in Paul's assuring the Roman Christians that to love one's fellow is a fulfilling of the Law; the implication of that is that if they are fulfilling other commands of the Law, but are being unloving, they are in fact being unfaithful to this central thrust of the Law. Conversely those who disparaged the keeping of the Law need to be reminded that love is its central thrust; love is at the centre of the message of the Christian gospel (Rom 5.5) and therefore they should not disparage this sort of Law-keeping. The argument here is thus rather similar to that employed by Paul in Gal 5.22-3, where, after listing the 'fruit' of God's spirit, he rather pointedly adds, with considerable under-statement, that 'against such (qualities) there is no law'; naturally, for the first of those qualities listed was, significantly, love, and just previously he had anticipated Rom 13.8-10 in speaking of the whole Law being fulfilled in (the keeping of) one commandment, to love one's neighbour (Gal 5.14). His opponents in Galatia evidently set great store by the keeping of the Law when they called upon his gentile converts there to complete and perfect their faith by being circumcised and keeping the Jewish Law; how could they then find fault, he argues, with qualities of life which in fact answered to the real nature and central purpose of the Law? Nearer at hand, he had earlier in Romans spoken of those living in accordance with God's spirit in fact realizing in their lives that which the Law rightfully requires (8.4); that rightful (or right-eous) requirement was above all the requirement of love, and the spirit of God within Christians imparted to them that love which was of the essence of the divine nature (5.5).

Perhaps no more needs to be said in this context about 13.11-14.23 which have been touched on earlier, but **15.1-13** requires further consideration. The section starts with Paul very clearly aligning himself with the 'strong', that is with the opposite group to the 'weak in faith' mentioned in 14.1: 'we, the strong, ought to bear the weaknesses of those who are not strong, and we ought not to please ourselves' (15.1), but rather to please our neighbours (v 2). Thus the problems and concerns dealt with in chapter 14 are very clearly carried over into the following chapter as Paul appeals for consideration of one's fellow Christians and their interests. That is in itself a very clear guide to the identity of the 'weak' and the 'strong' as respectively supporters of a Judaizing Christianity and of a non-Jewish Christianity, as Francis Watson has rightly noted, although he oversimplifies by speaking just of Jewish and gentile Christians (*Paul* 96). Moreover Paul's aligning himself with the 'strong' carries with it the implication that *the criticisms levelled against them by the weak, implied in chapter 14, would also be levelled against himself.*

In v 2 he picks up a further key term of 1 Corinthians, 'upbuilding, edification' (*oikodomē*).[7] 'Pleasing one's neighbours' means building them up, and in doing this Christians imitate Christ's self-denial and his renunciation of his own interests (15.3). Paul then cites Ps 69.9, 'the insults of those who insult thee have fallen on me' (*RSV*); some have found this choice of text an unhappy one.[8] It can readily be seen that bearing insults intended for, or directed ultimately at, another is an example of self-denial and not pleasing oneself, but nevertheless this was surely a relatively small part of Christ's self-denying suffering. This aspect of his passion is perhaps, however, singled out for mention because Paul and those in the Roman church who espoused his Law-free gospel and followed his lead had become the butt of insults, rebukes and accusations from both Jews and Judaizing Christians, critical alike of their freedom from the Law and of the immorality which they supposed to be the inevitable consequence of their jettisoning of the Law of Moses;[9] the consequent suffering inflicted upon Paul and his followers for the most part amounted to no more than bearing unwarranted accusations against their character and against the message which they preached and followed. Yet at times, it is true, the reaction of critics of the Law-free gospel must have taken a more violent form; Paul's reference in 2 Cor 11.24 to his having five times received the 39 lashes that could be inflicted by the synagogue authorities may well be an instance of this; the tumult in the synagogues referred to by Suetonius, it was suggested above, may well be another, and there was always the danger of resentment spilling over into physical violence. For the Law-free gospel, it may be suggested, was construed as a licence for immorality. Such a charge against God's message, Paul may well be implying here, is also a charge against the God who has acted in such a way as to bring this gospel into being. Just as those who rejected Jesus were rejecting the God in whose name he came and spoke and acted, so too those who vilified Paul's gospel and those who followed it were in fact criticizing the God who was its author.

If the Roman Christians would heed the Old Testament scriptures they would have hope, Paul continues (v 4). This linking of the bearing of suffering with hope recalls the argument earlier in 5.3-5, that a Christian's suffering is a cause for confidence, for it produces in the Christian powers of endurance and a tested character and thus hope. Here, rather than pointing the Christian towards his or her own character strengthened in the fires of suffering and towards the presence of God's spirit poured out powerfully in Christians' hearts, Paul points back to the Old Testament to the recurrent pattern of the suffering of God's faithful down the centuries. Hope and confidence are, we shall see, a theme that pervades the letter, and it is no accident that this word 'hope' recurs at this point, and rkturns again twice in 15.13 in the culmination of this section of Romans.

We saw earlier that 15.5 picks up another theme common, not to Romans as a whole, but to that section of it that starts at 12.1; this is the desire of Paul that they should think (*phronein*) in a way appropriate to their Christian calling. Here it is more specifically a thinking in the same way, having a common mind, enabling them to share together in extolling their God (v 6); implicit here is perhaps not only the idea that 'thinking according to Christ Jesus' will mean that they will not press their own interests, but also the idea that, if the one Christ truly controls their thinking, then he will bring them together into a harmony of purpose and outlook.

Both Jews and gentiles have cause to extol God, as one who has been faithful to the promises made to the Old Testament patriarchs (v 8) and one who has shown mercy to the nations (v 9). Christ has welcomed both Jews and gentiles (v 7),[10] and his followers should be no more choosy or stand-offish, no less welcoming of each other. Perhaps with an eye to the self-assertive 'strong' who wished to insist upon their freedom from the Law and criticized the 'weak' for not sharing it, Paul adds in 15.8 that Christ was a 'servant' to the circumcision; it may well be that in this description of Christ's role he seeks to show the 'strong' that they should be less eager to please themselves and more eager to 'serve' the circumcision themselves by doing nothing that made it harder for Jews to see God's glory manifested in the gospel of Christ; they should seek to build up their weaker brothers and sisters' faith in Christ rather than to alienate them from this faith.

To conclude this section of the chapter we can thus say that Paul's argument in 12.1-15.13 has come full circle back to the renewal of the Roman Christians' minds and thinking for which he appealed in 12.2. Renewed minds will be fashioned after the likeness of the Christ who did not seek his own interests (15.3); they will be no less welcoming and accepting of their fellows, be they Jew or gentile, than he was (15.7). Thus they will be able to live united and harmoniously in accord with the pattern manifested in Christ Jesus (15.5). This is a way that is pleasing to God and is truly the will of God (cf. 12.2), for it is a way that brings glory to their God (15.6-9); a people of God that includes gentiles is also very clearly God's will, for it was foretold in the Old Testament (15.9-12). In this way *12.2 may be said to introduce the main thrust of Paul's exhortations in Rom 12.1-15.13, a thrust that is highly relevant to, and directed towards, a specific situation in the Roman church.*

4. Romans 9.1-11.36 in Its Context

However, if that is the purpose of 12.1-15.13, how is it related to what precedes it, namely the main body of the letter with its extensive and sustained doctrinal argument? And how is that main body in turn related to what precedes it, in Paul's opening greetings to the Romans? To complete the argument of this study it is therefore necessary to try to discover the links that bind the main body of the letter, first to what follows it, and then to what precedes it. In other words we are here concerned with the links that bind the last section of 1.16-11.36, namely chapters 9-11, to the following exhortations. Then in the next chapter we must turn to the connection between 1.16ff and what precedes it, that is the thanksgiving which announces Paul's hoped for visit to Rome, as well as to the purpose within the context of the writing of Romans of that body of teaching which forms the bulk of the letter.

At the start of the previous section we had already briefly noted how 'by God's mercies' in 12.1 linked the following exhortations to the conclusion of the preceding argument: God's mercy had been a repeated theme of chapters 9-11. We saw, too, that in 12.1 Paul used a different word to that used in the previous three chapters to speak of God's mercy. In 12.8, however, the verb *eleeō*, 'I show mercy, am merciful', used in 9.15-16, 18 and 11.30-2, returns; furthermore the cognate noun *eleos*, found in 9.23 and 11.31, recurs in 15.9 at the close of this section of Romans. Paul there comes to speak of God's mercy manifested to the gentiles, and does so in the context of his appeal to the Roman Christians to accept and welcome one another. Judaizing Roman Christians, in other words, have no reason to find fault with adherents of the Law-free gospel, for, as chapters 9-11 have made abundantly clear, it is God's prerogative to show mercy as God chooses (cf., e.g., 9.15-17) and in fact the divine choice and decision is to show it to all (11.32).

On the other hand those who have followed the Law-free gospel have no cause to disparage Jewish or Judaizing Christians either, for they owe their own position and status as members of God's people to God's mercy alone. Indeed they should recall that they are being admitted into the privileges intended for God's chosen people (11.13ff); if God can show mercy even to non-Jews, it is all the easier for that same God to show mercy to the heirs of the original recipients of the divine promises. Any arrogant pride on the part of those who have cast off the Law as an encumbrance is quite out of place; a consciousness that one owes one's present position solely to God's mercy should make it impossible to suppose that any others, especially those so closely tied to the promises and purposes of God as the Jewish people were, were beyond the reach and grasp of that same mercy. If some respond to that mercy and acknowledge God's saving ways, but still cling to their traditional Jewish ways of life, that is no reason to deny them a share in God's mercy and grace; Christ has accepted them too, as Jews, and so should their gentile brothers and sisters in Christ.

So chapters 9-11 end with an appeal to those Christians who had shaken off the yoke of the Law to show respect towards the Jews and Jewish traditions, and to allow God to work according to the divine purpose and will in dealing with the people to whom such promises and such a spiritual inheritance had been given. This attitude and way of thinking, one according to that Christ who became a servant of the circumcision (15.8), finds a very apt application in the following appeal to the Roman Christians relating to the way in which they regarded those of their fellow-Christians there who were unwilling to break with Judaism and their distinctive Jewish way of life. But it also had a further relevance to 15.14ff and the project of the collection. For in that passage of Romans, it may be recalled, the reason given for the gentile Christians being under an obligation to assist the Jerusalem church materially was the fact that they had shared in the spiritual wealth of that church (15.27).

Now that spiritual wealth could certainly be interpreted simply as a reference to the fact that the early Christian movement originated in Palestine and that from the first Jerusalem seems to have been the centre of the earliest church; the first recipients of the Christian message there had not kept it to themselves, but had spread it abroad, so that in due course the gentiles came to hear it. But perhaps Paul has more in mind than just that. The gospel is, Paul asserts in Rom 1.16, God's power at work to bring about the salvation of all who believe, the Jew first of all and also the Greek. That 'first of all' may not just be an affirmation of what actually happened to be the case, that Jews did first experience that saving power at work in their midst, but also an affirmation of what had to be the case: it was right and fitting and necessary that they heard and experienced this first. In other words the preaching of the gospel in the midst of the Jewish people in their homeland was no historical accident; it had to be so if God was to remain faithful to the promises made to the patriarchs (15.8). For this was the people of the chosen race of Israel, adopted as God's children, sharing the divine glory, possessing the covenants, the divine Law, the cult and the promises (9.4); they were the descendants of the patriarchs, and Christ himself was one of them by physical descent (9.5; cf. 1.3). It was surely unthinkable that God's salvation should not be offered to them if God was at all faithful and consistent, unthinkable even that it should not be offered to them first of all, even if it was yet again only a meagre 'elected remnant' who responded to that offer (11.5), a remnant that included Paul himself (11.1), but also the Jerusalem church.

Using Paul's imagery of the olive-tree (cf. 11.17ff) we may thus say that an affirmation of fellowship with that church such as the collection was meant to be also meant an acknowledgment of indebtedness to the spiritual stock onto which the gentile Christians had been grafted. The Jerusalem church represented that growth of the original stock that had remained intact and had not been cut off in its stubbornness and hardness of heart. The spiritual wealth which was theirs and which they shared with the gentiles was not simply their possession of the Christian gospel and Christian tradition, but rather their possession of this tradition as a continuation of the true inheritance of the people of Israel. Their wealth did not begin with the coming of Christ, for they were at the same time heirs to the whole rich spiritual heritage of Israel, forming God's faithful elected remnant in the present time like the seven thousand that had not given allegiance to Baal in Elijah's time. They had realized in their persons the destiny of Israel (11.2-7).

Thus an understanding of God's ways of working and of the special position of Israel within that working was not only meant, in Paul's argument, to lead those gentile Christians at Rome who were inclined to despise their Judaizing fellow Christians there to be more tolerant of their clinging to Jewish traditions. It was also meant to lead them to a new awareness of the special place in God's purpose of that small body of Jewish Christians and above all of the mother-church in Jerusalem; to renounce their indebtedness to the Christian community in Jerusalem was to cut themselves off from the stock onto which God had grafted them; it would be as if branches could exist suspended in mid air with no main stem or trunk to support them.

When the second half of Romans is viewed in this light it can thus be seen that there is an integral relationship between the themes of chapters 9-11 and the twofold appeal issued by Paul in the subsequent chapters, firstly to be renewed in their thinking so that they might see (and do) what served God's purposes and the interests of their fellow Christians, and secondly to align themselves, and identify themselves, with Paul's journey to Jerusalem to bring the collection to the church there. That renewal of their minds would be shown in a new appreciation of the legitimacy of Israel's heritage in the Christian church; if some saw the preservation of that heritage necessitating a continued loyalty to the Jewish Law they should seek to appreciate that position, and welcome those who adopted it, just as the Judaizing Christians should recognize the validity of the presence in God's people of gentiles who remained gentiles and did not become Jews. Both groups remained dependent upon one thing alone, God's mercy. Nor, secondly, should the obduracy and hostility towards the gospel of the majority of Jews blind the Roman Christians to the vital role that the small group of Christians in Jerusalem had played, not only in mediating to them the Christian gospel, but also as embodying for them Israel's spiritual heritage into which they had been privileged to enter.

Yet, if chapters 9-11 can thus be shown to have a direct relevance to those things which Paul saw to be wrong, or in danger of being wrong, in the Roman Christians' attitudes and conduct, and which he sought to change or guard against by writing his letter, can the same be said of the first eight chapters? To that question we must now turn.

V

THE ARGUMENT OF ROMANS 1-11 IN ITS CONTEXT

In the first chapter of this study (§1) we saw that Ulrich Luz criticized recent attempts to expound Romans as a response to a particular concrete situation; these attempts came to grief, he argued, in their failure to make sense of the argument of the body of the letter, and above all chapters 1-8 (cf. Williams, '"Righteousness"' 245). Rather, he holds, Paul argues against the Jews and their way to salvation, rather than addressing directly the predominantly gentile recipients of the letter. As we saw, Luz's view is that the structure of the argument of Romans grows out of its subject-matter ('Aufbau' 162f).

That challenges those who seek to explain Romans as addressing a particular situation to offer some explanation of the first eight or eleven chapters in the light of that postulated situation. Unless they can do that they can only claim to have given an explanation for part of the letter, and a relatively small part of it at that. At the same time one might also ask two questions of Luz's account:

(1) Is it not also pertinent to ask why this particular choice of subject-matter is discussed in the letter to the Romans? If, for instance, the subject being discussed there were the Jewish way to salvation as Luz suggests, would one not also have to ask why that was of interest to, or thought by Paul to be particularly relevant to, a predominantly gentile church? And if one explains Paul's choice by, for example, appealing to the presence of large numbers of Jews in Rome is one not then also positing a concrete particular situation in Rome to explain the choice of topics discussed?

(2) Is the argument of these chapters in fact correctly described as a debate with the Jews and their way to salvation rather than, say, a defence against the Jews' criticisms of the way of salvation proclaimed by Paul? As the argument of this chapter progresses it will, I hope, become clear that the latter characterization is a more apt description of what Paul is doing in this letter.

Fundamental to any consideration of this question is the first chapter of Romans where Paul moves from material that is clearly addressed to a particular group of people, the Christians at Rome, to material which seems not to have any special reference to them and their situation, and therefore it is necessary to pay especial attention to this part of the letter where the specific epistolary framework of the letter, which quite clearly addresses this particular group of people in their situation, connects with an argument that seems to be completely abstracted from any such particular context (cf. Zeller, *Juden* 39). But first Paul's opening greetings deserve close attention, the more so since Kettunen argues that it is Paul's practice to express his most important concerns at this point in his letters (*Abfassungszweck* 50).

1. The Opening Greeting (Rom 1.1-7)

The opening greeting of Romans is an unusual one. In the first place it follows the basic pattern and structure of Paul's opening greetings in his other letters, but differs from them in its length. Apart from Romans the longest opening greeting of a Pauline letter is to be found in 1 Cor 1.1-3, but that is little over half the length of the greeting in Romans. The likeliest cause of this is the unusual situation in which Paul was placed in writing Romans, in that he was here writing to a church that he had neither founded nor visited previously;[1] moreover it was argued above that in this church Paul and his message were a matter of considerable controversy. In such a situation considerable care and tact were called for, and that was above all the case with the all-important opening lines of the letter which would create an initial impression amongst the recipients, either favourable or unfavourable. Moreover, because he was unknown to some, or indeed perhaps many, of the Christians in Rome Paul must introduce himself with greater care and explicitness than was usually necessary. He has to set out his credentials more fully, and this largely accounts for the greater length of his initial greeting.

The same situation, of writing to a church that was not founded by him or his fellow-workers, may also account for a number of other features of this passage. In the first place it is widely accepted that in 1.3-4 Paul quotes a piece of traditional credal material:

[... his Son,]

who was descended from (*ek*) David according to (*kata*) the flesh

and designated Son of God in power according to (*kata*) the Spirit of holiness by (*ek*) his resurrection from the dead, [Jesus Christ our Lord ...] (*RSV*).

That this is a quotation is rendered plausible by a number of features of this passage:

(a) In form it is a self-contained unit which could easily be removed from the text without any dislocation. Indeed the repetition of 'his Son ... designated Son of God' is rather awkward, particularly if the first mention of Jesus' sonship most probably presupposes the usual Pauline view that Jesus was already God's son when he was sent into the world (cf., e.g., Gal 4.4), but the second seems to give the impression that Jesus' sonship began with his resurrection; this impression can only really be overcome by stressing the words 'in power'; then what is inaugurated at his resurrection is not his sonship as such, but his sonship 'in power'.

(b) Moreover this passage is made up of two roughly parallel lines, even if the second is considerably longer than the first and the prepositional phrases introduced by *ek* and *kata* are in a different order in each case. There are a number of similar passages in the New Testament that are often, even generally, regarded as quotations of traditional material. For instance a longer passage, 1 Tim 3.16, is often printed in editions and translations in the form of verse; moreover, like Rom 1.3-4, its first two lines contain a contrast of 'flesh' and 'spirit'.

(c) A number of terms and ideas are found here which are unusual in Paul's writings; for instance we have here 'the spirit of holiness' instead of Paul's usual 'holy spirit', and the phrase 'by his resurrection from the dead' is literally 'from (since, by) resurrection of dead (people)', which is not only unusual for Paul but decidedly odd as well, in that it might at first sight seem to be speaking of a general resurrection of dead people in the plural rather than simply of Jesus' resurrection.

Cumulatively, then, the evidence for a quotation of non-Pauline material here is strong. But why does he quote it here? One plausible reason is that this was a credal affirmation which the Roman Christians would recognize as such, and would recognize as an important part of the content of the Christian message which they had received and accepted. One could indeed argue that the somewhat adoptionist-sounding language of v 4, which could be construed as saying that the man Jesus became exalted to be God's son after his resurrection, might well stem from the creed of a Christianity that was strongly coloured by Jewish beliefs and practices, and we saw above that this may well have been the sort of version of the Christian faith that first took root in Rome. Certainly later Jewish Christian groups were often adoptionist in their Christology.[2] It has in fact been argued that the words 'in power' were a later addition, by Paul or someone before him, to avoid this suggestion of adoptionism; certainly there is no prepositional 'in' phrase in v 3 that corresponds to it, whereas both verses have otherwise each one prepositional phrase introduced by *ek* and one introduced by *kata*. Even thus qualified and glossed, however, the declaration would be recognizable as an affirmation of the faith in Christ which the Roman Christians had received, and Paul could then be citing it as evidence that he was a messenger in the service of the same Lord whom the Christians in Rome acknowledged and served.

It is in keeping with this that Paul, at least in the opinion of some, cites traditional Christian material unusually frequently in Romans. Kettunen, for instance, points to 3.24-6; 4.17, 24-5; 5.6, 8; 6.4, 9; 7.4; 8.3, 11, 15, 29-30, 32, 34, 37; 10.9 and 14.9, 15 besides this passage (*Abfassungszweck* 176). Now a glance at commentaries will rapidly show that not all would accept that these are in fact quotations of, or even allusions to, tradition; I myself would not agree to all of this list of references, but nevertheless I feel that a strong enough case can be made out for enough of them to justify Kettunen's further claim that Paul thus appeals to traditions because of his concern to show that his gospel is in line with that of the rest of the church (cf. Michel, *Röm* 4-5). Moreover, the fact that he has to demonstrate that to a church which was in part at least very much steeped in Jewish traditions (chapter 3 §2) may explain why he introduces himself as the 'slave' or 'servant of Christ Jesus' (1.1); for it seems likely that the titular sense of 'Christ' ('anointed one', 'Messiah') would be more strongly felt when the term was placed before the name 'Jesus' (cf. W. Grundmann in *TDNT* 6, 542; Cranfield, *Rom* [ICC] 1, 51), and that would be appropriate when Paul was addressing a congregation part of which was keenly aware that the Jesus in whom they had placed their trust was the anointed one expected by Jews. The same circumstances will also partly explain the considerable use made later in this letter of quotations of, and arguments from, the Old Testament; this is by no means always the case, as can be seen from a comparison with a letter like 1 Thessalonians.

It is understandable, too, that, if his right to be regarded as an apostle is open to question in Rome, Paul stresses more than usually his divine call to his apostleship. But it is not a little interesting also that he so stresses that his apostolic ministry is to be 'among all the nations', especially when he adds in 1.6 that his Roman readers were amongst those nations. For by implication that means that he is *their* apostle too and therefore responsible for them; but it is only implied, for it would have been rash of him to state this too explicitly if his credentials and message were being questioned by some in Rome, and if he could not in their case point to the very existence of the church there as evidence of his divine commission (contrast 1 Cor 9.1-2).

One final point to note is that he greets 'all' the Christians in Rome (1.7). It is not that he writing simply to a group of his own supporters amongst the Christians in Rome; he writes to all whether they support him and acknowledge his authority or not. His message in this letter, in other words, is for both 'strong' and 'weak' in the church there.

THE REASONS FOR ROMANS

2. Paul's Stated Purposes in Writing Romans

It is one of the great strengths of Kettunen's study that it pays particular attention to a couple of brief explicit, or almost explicit, indications that Paul gives of his purposes in writing to the Romans and of what he hoped to achieve by so writing. These indications he finds in certain phrases in chapters 1 and 15:

(1) 'I desire to see you, that I may share some spiritual gift with you in order that you may be strengthened' (1.11). This verse, however, can only be indirect evidence of Paul's purpose in writing; it is indirect in that one has to assume both that Paul's present purpose in his plans to visit Rome and his purpose in writing the letter largely coincide, as Kettunen does (e.g. *Abfassungszweck* 146), and that the writing of the letter serves the same purpose as the visit that Paul was desirous of making (cf. ibid. 147); the former would thus be a substitute, at least temporarily, for the latter. Then one can argue that in writing his letter Paul was discharging his apostolic task of furthering their faith. For, if he was responsible to bring about 'the obedience of faith', i.e. the obedience which faith is, the obedience that is inherent in faith (1.5), amongst all the gentiles, then he was responsible, Kettunen argues (ibid. 138), not just for bringing them to faith, but also for keeping them faithful to the gospel. What is not clear from this, however, is precisely what 'spiritual gift' was thus being imparted to the Roman Christians in the writing of this letter. One might plausibly think here of the 'mystery' which Paul imparts in Rom 11.25ff: a partial 'hardening' has come upon Israel until the full number of the gentiles has been gathered in. Kettunen, however, rightly points to the comparable language to that of 1.11 used by Paul of his initial evangelism in Thessalonica ('to share ... the gospel', 1 Thess 2.8), but now in the context of Romans such language is more problematic unless 'sharing the gospel' and 'preaching the gospel' are not solely activities relevant to the founding of a church, but are also necessary for keeping it in being and keeping it faithful to its calling. That same problem arises again in 1.15, for there too Paul speaks of preaching the gospel to the Roman church ('you'), and it

is hard to be convinced that Kettunen is right to take this of the past, before the Roman church was founded.[3]

However, that problem apart, *it is clear from 1.11 that Paul feels himself responsible to further the Romans' faith, whether by a personal visit or by letter, and that is evidence of his conviction that he was their apostle too and pastorally responsible for them.* This much is clear from this verse and that is a valuable clue to Paul's frame of mind in writing the letter.

However, if we only had the evidence of this verse, that would hardly warrant any inferences about Paul's purpose in writing the letter, since it primarily speaks of a purpose that Paul had in desiring to visit the Romans. (And Kettunen does complicate matters by arguing that differences between chapter 1 and chapter 15 are to be explained by the fact that Paul hoped that the situation would be altered by the receipt of his letter. In that case we have the purpose which Paul would have had if he had been able to visit Rome earlier – to found the church there, according to Kettunen – his purpose had he visited it then and his purpose in writing the letter, which would be the same, and, finally, his purpose in visiting it when he eventually was able to do so, after his Jerusalem visit and after his letter had done its work.)

(2) However this is not the only evidence that we have: Kettunen observes that it is odd how little attention **15.15** has received in accounts of the purpose of Romans (ibid. 150). In this verse and the following one Paul states that

> on some points I have written to you very boldly by way of a reminder, because of the grace given to me by God to be a servant of Christ Jesus to the gentiles, performing the sacred service of proclaiming the gospel of God, in order that my offering of the gentiles [i.e. my offering which is the gentiles, the gentile converts] might be acceptable [to God], consecrated by [God's] holy spirit.

What is immediately clear in this passage is that it confirms the impression given implicitly in Paul's opening greetings to the Romans that he was claiming that his apostolic commission had made him responsible for the Roman Christians too. Otherwise it is hard to explain why the grace of his calling to be an apostle to the gentiles should be offered as an explanation for his boldness in writing to them. Because God's grace has made him responsible for them too as a gentile church he has taken it upon himself to write thus to them on some matters.

Kettunen argues that Paul is here confronted with a dilemma: he must perform his service to the church in Jerusalem, but the situation in Rome demands his attention also; this dilemma he solves for the time being by writing to the Romans and proceeding with his visit to Jerusalem. Paul's purpose in writing is one of reminding, rather than exhorting or correcting; the Romans should know that his opponents' accusations are malicious slanders, for Paul's gospel is in harmony with Christian tradition (ibid. 152-4). It is, however, doubtful whether one needs to postulate, as it becomes clearer later that Kettunen does (see esp. ibid. 182-6), the presence in Rome of Judaizing opponents in the form of a counter-mission such as one finds in Galatia, where Paul roundly condemns those proclaiming 'another gospel' there (Gal 1.6-8). If the Roman church was originally established on a Judaizing basis, with a form of Christianity that had not broken free from the synagogue and from obedience to the Jewish Law, then it would be only too natural that rumours and reports about Paul's message would fall on hostile ears in certain circles of the Roman church. It is true that there was the danger of those who preached another, Judaizing gospel coming to Rome and therefore finding a ready hearing there; consequently Paul warns the Romans to look out for such people (16.17), but that does not necessarily entail that they had already arrived there; indeed it perhaps makes better sense if they had not.

Paul's message to the Romans may certainly be described as a reminder, but it is doubtful whether this ought to be contrasted with exhortation or correction as Kettunen does; he is perhaps led to do this by his conviction that the problem which Paul had in the Roman church was not with Roman Christians but with outsiders. After all, to recall someone to what they have learnt in the past may well serve to exhort or correct them if they are falling short or departing from what they learnt previously. That he chooses this word 'remind' does, however, again imply that he sees what he is saying to them, not as the imparting of some new gospel, but as reinforcing and continuing the message which they had received before. Whether it was in fact the same as they had all received before is, of course, another matter; if the form of the Christian tradition originally received in Rome was of a Judaizing character then it is unlikely that it matched Paul's message in all respects; Paul would be likely to be aware of that, but it suited his strategy to appeal to them as the authoritative representative of a shared Christian tradition, common to him and to themselves.[4]

Paul, however, admits that he has been 'very bold' in some of the things which he has written to them. That implies that he is conscious that some of the things which he has said will have been hard for his readers to accept; part of his message at least is highly controversial at Rome. We have already seen arguments to the effect that Paul himself and what he stood for were controversial there. That element of controversy has evidently not been avoided entirely in what he now writes to them. We have also seen that what he goes on to say about the collection journey to Jerusalem was probably a source of considerable disagreement, and earlier his advice to the 'weak' and the 'strong' in 14.1-15.13 was doubtless also hard for some of them to take: did it not involve a compromising both of the freedom of the 'strong' and of the purity of the 'weak' if the former must allow the legitimacy of a Christian life-style that seemed to be in bondage to the Jewish Law and the latter had to acknowledge impure gentiles as fellow-Christians? But perhaps, too, some of the things said earlier in the letter touched on raw nerves; this is a question that will have to be borne in mind in the rest of this chapter, and particularly when we come to consider the theme of 'God's righteousness'.

There are also other references in chapter 15 to what Paul hoped to experience in Rome when he visited that church *en route* to Spain. He hoped to see them and to be at least in part 'filled with them' (v 24). This 'filling' Kettunen plausibly takes to be a reference, not to material aid, but to Paul's satisfying himself that the Romans are obedient to the gospel, and that their faith is in good order (ibid. 164). Seen in that light, the reference in v 32 to Paul's being 'refreshed' by his time amongst them may be less a matter of the relaxing vacation which some English translations may suggest that it was to be (e.g. *NEB* : 'enjoy a time of rest'), and more a matter of Paul's being encouraged and relieved by the state in which he hopes to find the Roman church; he hopes, that is, that, after the encouragement which he also hopes to receive from a successful visit to Jerusalem with the collection, he will receive further encouragement by finding the Roman church as he would have it.

At this point Kettunen makes the further suggestion that Paul introduces the matter of the collection here because the success of this project would mean a recognition of Paul's apostleship and of the gentile Christians whom he had won by his preaching. That may be true, but he also needed to explain why he was not visiting the Roman Christians immediately if he had so long desired to do so, and, as we have seen, he also desired their backing for the collection. Both of these are more natural reasons for his mention of the collection here, and both are more clearly suggested by the text. Kettunen, though, sees that the Romans would not have supported Paul's collection project nor would they have supported him in prayer if they had held a distorted, unfavourable view of him; therefore Paul's request had to be preceded by a defence of his gospel (ibid. 175). So too Dahl suggests that

> The appeal for intercession may, indeed, be a main reason why Paul wrote *this* letter to the Romans. The Christians in Rome needed to know what Paul taught and how he understood his own mission if they were going to ally themselves with other Pauline churches and intercede for a favorable reception of the collection. ('Theology' 77)

Equally, one could say that that defence, and a successful one at that, would be necessary if Paul's visit to them was indeed going to be an occasion for refreshment and encouragement, rather than a strenuous time of rebutting charges and accusations. At this point, therefore, we come near to finding an explanation for the lengthy exposition of Paul's message that occupies so much of the letter from 1.18 onwards.

Yet first it is necessary to ask why Paul could not have avoided this need to to defend himself simply by leaving the Roman

Christians to themselves. Why did he need to write to them or to visit them at all? Why could he not proceed straight to Spain? If he needed to travel there via Rome because that was the easiest route would there then be any need to embroil himself in passing with the church there if that was likely to be so contentious an encounter? After all Beker suggests (*Paul* 72) that Paul would not even have visited Rome but for his plans to go to Spain. If it was a matter of financial and material assistance could that not be gained more easily from those churches on whose support he could count? One good reason why he could not take this easier path of least resistance we have already seen: he regarded the Roman church as his responsibility, within his allotted sphere of operations. And in fact that may have been his major reason for going there, and thus for preparing the way in writing, rather than any pressing need to have the church there as a base of operations for his Spanish mission or to have their material backing or their moral and spiritual support for that mission.[5] Rome was part of that mission field which God had entrusted to him and therefore he could not ignore it or leave it alone.

3. The Forthcoming Visit to Rome and the Body of the Letter

Kettunen also argues (*Abfassungszweck* 113-15) that the expression used at the start of 1.13, 'I do not wish you to be ignorant ...', is one of a group of expressions frequently used by Paul to introduce important matters of which, as the words suggest, he does not want his readers to remain unaware; in other words he chooses to make it explicit and clear that what follows is a piece of information to which they must pay particular heed.[6]

In this case the piece of information that is put to them so emphatically is Paul's long-standing, but often frustrated, desire to visit them in order to have a fruitful ministry among them as amongst the other gentiles. He desires to preach the gospel amongst them as he does amongst all the other gentiles (1.15).[7] That leads him on to a brief pronouncement on the nature of the gospel in 1.16-17 which in turn launches him on a detailed theological argument the like of which is found in no other letter of his.

We can see from this that these verses in the middle of chapter 1 serve as a link binding together the opening greetings and thanksgiving and the ensuing doctrinal section. The former are very closely tied to the situation of the Roman church and in particular to Paul's relationship with them and, by implication, their attitude to him, but the latter, which occupies so major a part of the letter, on the surface seems, as we have seen from so many scholars' judgments on it, to have relatively little connection with Paul's relations with Rome or the Roman Christians' view of him. The former section, therefore, is very 'situation-oriented', the latter seems at first sight to be divorced from any particular situation.

Verses 16 and 17 in particular are often regarded as setting the theme for the subsequent doctrinal exposition. So Cranfield heads his commentary on vv 16*b* -17 'The theme of the epistle is stated' (*Rom* 1, 87), and Käsemann simply labels his discussion of 16 and 17 'Theme' (*Thema – Röm* 18). It is therefore understandable that Barrett had earlier concluded that 'Most commentators recognize in them [vv 16 and 17] the "text" of the epistle; it is not wrong to see in them a summary of Paul's theology as a whole' (*Rom* 27; the second statement seems to me to go too far). In the light of this these two verses are obviously of especial importance for our enquiry both by virtue of their being on this borderline between the 'situation-oriented' opening section and the following doctrinal section that is seemingly not oriented to any particular situation, let alone that which is the theme of the thanksgiving, and by virtue of its introductory or programmatic role in relation to the section which follows.

It is significant that Cranfield takes the first part of v 16 with the preceding passage, and that others take both verses in their entirety with the preceding section (so recently the commentaries of Wilckens and Zeller). There is no clear-cut division between them and what goes before (nor, for that matter, between them and what follows, for v 17 is parallel to, and linked with, v 18). Thus v 16 is immediately connected with Paul's declared desire to preach the gospel in Rome also. It provides a reason for the desire, linked to v 15 by a causal conjunction 'for' (*gar*), since Paul explains in it that he is not put to shame by the gospel which he preaches or by his preaching of the gospel.[8] That is a connection that makes far better sense if *some in Rome had in fact claimed that he indeed ought to be ashamed of his gospel and his proclamation, for that gospel was in some way discredited and disgraceful.* It will be the argument of the rest of this chapter that that had been claimed, and that *the argument of the rest of Romans from this point to the end of chapter 11 is a defence of Paul's message and ministry against charges which claimed that it was indeed shameful.*

Jewett saw the language of 1.16 as political in nature: it expresses the confidence of an envoy who knows that the sovereign whom he or she represents is powerful enough to prevail against the opposing forces ('Romans' 15). He prefers this setting to those interpretations that regard Paul's language as reflecting the setting of an eschatological lawsuit or trial; such an interpretation was that preferred by Gerhard Herold (*Zorn*). Against this latter view is the apparently present tense of 'I am not ashamed'; must one then say that Paul is confident now because he is confident of future vindication when God's will and judgment on the world is finally revealed? (Herold in fact gives this present tense a future sense, 'I will not be put to shame by the gospel' – ibid. 229) But that is to overlook the fact that Paul talks here in the language of 'realized eschatology': he speaks of a revelation of God's righteousness now, in the present, and a revelation of God's wrath now from heaven. These revelations were both things that Paul's Jewish contemporaries would have expected to have occurred in the future and to mark the end when the divine purpose and nature would finally be revealed for all to see, a revelation that would be at one and the same time salvation for some, but judgment and condemnation to others. If Paul here speaks of these usually future events as things of the present there may be no need to choose between the political background of Paul's language and that of Jewish eschatology, or between the 'now' of the former and the still future 'then' of the latter. There is now taking place, Paul is claiming, the disclosure of the power of that sovereign whom Paul serves, and whose ambassador he is, and Paul is not being put to shame, losing face, in the service of his God; the disclosure of the power of God in Paul's preaching is, at the same time, an eschatological act, in the sense of a final, irrevocable act after which no further, more ultimate or final disclosure is necessary or possible, however paradoxical that claim might seem amidst a world in which evil was still apparently all too rampant.

At the same time Paul is enough of a realist to appreciate that God's world and the human race is still in the grip of alien and hostile forces. Despite all the finality of what has happened in Jesus Christ (compare the perfect tense of 'has been manifested' in 3.21) and of what is happening now in the preaching of the gospel (treating the present tense of v 17, and of v 18, as a continuous present, 'is being revealed') Paul remains conscious that the reality of that happening is disclosed only to faith and is apprehended only by faith. Our salvation is not 'seen', it is a matter of hope, as he later puts it (8.24-5).

Consequently, as was already noted above (in chap. 4 §3), a further prominent theme of Romans is that of '**hope**'. It is one that is integrally related to Paul's affirmation in 1.16 that he is not being put to shame. Not only does the present manifestation of God's power prevent that, but so too does the still future making visible to all of the salvation which God has brought about and is at present effecting through the preaching of Paul. Paul is not discredited, because the God who is at work in his preaching is at work now, and is at work effectively, and also will bring that work to its conclusion in a manner that will be manifest to all. Thus not only does he round off the argument of 12.1-15.13 with a reference to the hope that the gentiles have in the promised descendant of Jesse (15.12) and the hope that should consequently abound in his readers (15.13), but, as we noted, the Old Testament scriptures should also be a source of hope, as his readers detected there the prevailing pattern of the suffering and the rejection that was the lot of God's faithful down the ages (15.4).

Earlier, in the main doctrinal exposition of the letter, 'hope' was equally prominent: Abraham's faith was an example of hope, for his faith that he would be the 'father of many nations' was a hope in the seemingly hopeless (4.18). Creation, subjected to futility, yet has the hope of liberation from bondage (8.20-1), and Christians too are 'saved on the basis of hope' (8.24), for the hoped-for salvation is not yet visible, but must be waited for patiently (8.25).

The term 'patiently' here represents the adverbial phrase *di' hypomonēs* in 8.25; the same term *hypomonē*, 'patience, patient endurance', recurs in the context of suffering (*thlipsis*) and hope (*elpis*) both in 12.12 and in another passage that was touched on earlier, 5.2-5. In the latter, as we saw, Paul speaks of suffering being a source of confident hope for Christians, for it schools them in this 'patient endurance', which in turn produces in them a tested character, tried in the fires of affliction, and that in its turn results in hope. That hope, he continues, does not disappoint us or put us to shame, for God's love has been poured out in our hearts through the indwelling holy spirit which has been given to us (5.5). The link with 1.16 is the clearer in that another compound of the same verb as is there translated 'I am not ashamed, I am not being put to shame' is used here to express the conviction that Christians' hope does not disappoint them, let them down or cause them to be put to shame in the sense that they are shown to have placed their hope in something worthless and illusory (*epaischynomai*, 1.16; *kataischynei*, 5.5). That idea in 5.5 must also be interpreted in the light of chapter 8, as is the case with many of the ideas introduced in 5.1-11 (see below). There this spirit that Christians experience poured out in their hearts is spoken of as a first-fruits (*aparchē*), an anticipation and foretaste of a future reality and also at the same time a reason for confidence in the eventual consummation of that future reality in all its fullness.

Rom 5.2 and 5.3 also link the theme of 'hope' to another term that is relevant to the present section of this chapter, the verb *kauchaomai* and its cognates. This is a most elusive word or group of words to translate, for it can be used pejoratively by Paul to describe a misplaced confidence, often translated as 'boasting', as well as positively of a well-founded confidence. On the one hand he speaks of those placing their reliance (*kauchaomai*) on (the observance of) the Jewish Law (2.23; in 2.19 he spoke of their confidence that they were guides to the blind, using a practically synonymous term, *pepoitha*); had Abraham been justified by his works he would have a reason for boasting or confidence in them (*kauchēma*, 4.2), but Paul will argue that God's action in Christ and the appropriate response of faith leave no room for such boasting or misplaced confidence (*kauchēsis*, 3.27; we have to supply the 'misplaced' here, or otherwise Paul seems to contradict himself in 5.2-3, 11). On the other hand the Jew relies on the Law (another synonym, *epanapauomai*, is used here) and has confidence (*kauchaomai*) in God according to 2.17; whereas Paul reckons the former misplaced, he could hardly find fault with the latter as such (similarly he could not fault his fellow-Jews for their 'zeal for God' as such in 10.2; the problem was that it was not an enlightened, *kat' epignōsin*, zeal), for Christians base their confidence in God too, but in their case this is mediated through Christ (5.11; cf. 1 Cor 1.31); in Christ he himself has confidence (*kauchēsis*) with regard to his service of God (15.17; cf. Jewett, 'Romans' 16-17). And, as we saw, in 5.2-3 Paul speaks of the grounds for Christians' confidence in their hope of God's glory and even in their experience of suffering.

The centrality of this theme of 'hope and confidence' to the argument of Romans is hard to deny, following as it does upon his confident initial declaration of his confidence in his gospel in the programmatic words of 1.16-17. It is no accident either, in my view, that the argument of the first eight chapters reaches its crescendo in another ringing declaration of Paul's conviction and confidence in 8.38-9:

> For I am convinced (here the term is *pepeismai*) that neither death nor life nor angels nor rulers nor present things nor things to come nor (supernatural) powers nor height nor depth nor any other creature will be able to separate us from God's love that is (found) in Christ Jesus our Lord.

It is no wonder that Paul can assert that the preaching of such a gospel does not put him to shame, does not cause him to lose face or be found wanting. This is the message that he triumphantly proclaims to the Roman Christians. At the same time the fact that he asserts this ultimate ground for his confidence to lie in the final judgment and declaration of God's verdict upon those who have put their trust in God's Son who will on that occasion take his place at God's right hand (8.34) is further confirmation that in 1.16 we should not exclude the eschatological dimension to Paul's declaration of confidence, however many present grounds for confidence he may also have; they are but, as it were, the foretaste, the first-fruits, of a coming vindication of God's messenger.

At the end of the previous section we saw that Kettunen argued that the Roman Christians could not support the collection or pray for Paul's success if they held an unfavourable view of him and his work, and I added that such an unfavourable view, if it was still held by the Roman Christians when Paul came to visit them, would make his planned visit to Rome an occasion for strenuous effort, even discomfort and distress, rather than one for refreshing encouragement as he hoped. Hence the need for his defence, a defence that was needed then, at that moment in time, if they were to back him in his collection journey, and which, if made successfully then, would surely make all the easier his planned pastoral visit to them after his journey to Jerusalem. But that in turn raises again the question why this defence should have been necessary at all, and why it took the form that it did.

4. The 'Righteousness of God'

Why should Paul have been ashamed of his gospel? What was it that his critics brought against it? It is at this point that the theme of '(God's) righteousness' may give us a clue. It is introduced in 1.17, but this language too, as was the case with the theme of 'hope and confidence' looked at in the last section, appears with a relatively very high frequency within the argument of the first eleven chapters of Romans, if we include both the noun 'righteousness' (*dikaiosynē*), both with and without the qualifying genitive 'of God', and also its cognates (the nouns *dikaiōma* and *dikaiōsis*, the verb *dikaioō*, usually translated 'justify', and the adjective *dikaios*) as well as its opposite 'unrighteous(ness)' (*adikia, adikos*); this suggests that this too is a central theme in the argument of this part of the letter.

The frequency of the occurrence of this terminology can be seen from the following instances (in order to make it easier to locate the following quotations, I have tried to keep as close as possible to the wording of the *RSV*, although I have departed from its translation in a number of places and for various reasons):

1.17: For in it [Paul's gospel] the righteousness (*dikaiosynē*) of God is being revealed ...; as it is written, 'He who through faith is righteous (*dikaios*) shall live' [Hab 2.4]. (18) For the wrath of God is being revealed ... against all ... wickedness (*adikia*) of the human race which by its wickedness (*adikia*) suppresses the truth.

1.29: they were filled with all manner of wickedness (*adikia* [perhaps not accidentally placed first in a whole list of vices]).

1.32: they know God's decree (*dikaiōma*) that those who do such things deserve to die ... .

2.8: those who ... obey wickedness (*adikia*).

2.13: For it is not the hearers of the Law who are righteous (*dikaios*) before God, but the doers of the Law who will be justified (*dikaioō*).

2.26: if one who is uncircumcised keeps the precepts (*dikaiōma* [here in the plural as opposed to the singular of 1.32]) of the Law ... .

3.4: 'That you [God] may be justified (*dikaioō*) in your words ...' [Ps 51.4 (50.6 LXX)]. (5) But if our wickedness (*adikia*) serves to show the justice (*dikaiosynē*) of God, what shall we say? That God is unjust (*adikos*) ...?

3.10: 'None is righteous (*dikaios*) ...' [Ps 14.1].

3.20: no human being will be justified (*dikaioō*) in God's sight by works of the Law ... . (21) Now the righteousness (*dikaiosynē*) of God has been manifested apart from the Law ... , (22) the righteousness (*dikaiosynē*) of God through the faith(fulness) of Jesus Christ ... .[9]

3.24: they are justified (*dikaioō*) by God's grace ... .

3.25: This was to show God's righteousness (*dikaiosynē*) ... (26) to show God's righteousness in the present time, so that God might be righteous (*dikaios*) even when[10] justifying (*dikaioō*) the one whose life is based on the faith(fulness) of Jesus.

3.28: a person is justified (*dikaioō*) by faith ... .

3.30: God will justify (*dikaioō*) the uncircumcised ... .

4.2: if Abraham was justified (*dikaioō*) by works ... .

4.3: 'it was reckoned to him as righteousness (*dikaiosynē*)' [Gen 15.6; cf. the allusions to this same Genesis text in Rom 4.5-6, 9, 11, 22, not all of which are quoted below].

4.5: to one ... who trusts the God who justifies (*dikaioō*) the ungodly, that person's faith is reckoned as righteousness (*dikaiosynē*).

4.11: He received circumcision as ... a seal of the righteousness (*dikaiosynē*) which he had by faith ... to make him the father of all ... who thus have righteousness (*dikaiosynē*) reckoned to them.

4.13: The promise to Abraham ...[came] ... through the righteousness (*dikaiosynē*) of faith.

4.25: [Jesus] who was raised for our justification (*dikaiōsis*).

5.1: we are justified (*dikaioō*) by faith.

5.7: one will hardly die for a righteous (*dikaios*) person.

5.9: we are now justified (*dikaioō*) by his [Christ's] blood.

5.16: ... the free gift following many trespasses brings justification (a verdict of acquittal, *dikaiōma*). (17) ... those who receive ... the free gift of righteousness (*dikaiosynē*) [will] reign ... . (18) one person's act of righteousness (*dikaiōma*) leads to acquittal (*dikaiōsis*) and life for all people. (19) ... many will be made righteous (*dikaios*).

5.21: grace abounded through righteousness (*dikaiosynē*) ... .

6.7: the one who has died is freed (*dikaioō*) from sin.

6.13: Do not yield your limbs to sin as instruments of wickedness (*adikia*), but yield ... your limbs to God as instruments of righteousness (*dikaiosynē*).

6.16: ... obedience, which leads to righteousness (*dikaiosynē*).

6.18: ... [you] have become slaves of righteousness (*dikaiosynē*). (19) ... yield your limbs to righteousness (*dikaiosynē*) for sanctification. (20) ... you were free in regard to righteousness (*dikaiosynē*)... .

7.12: the commandment is ... just (*dikaios*) ... .

8.4: the just requirement (*dikaiōma*) of the Law ... fulfilled in us ... .

8.10: but the spirit is life because of righteousness (*dikaiosynē*).[11]

8.30: those whom God called God also justified (*dikaioō*); and those whom God justified (*dikaioō*) God also glorified.

8.33: It is God who justifies (*dikaioō*).

9.14: Is there injustice (*adikia*) on God's part?

9.31: Israel pursued the righteousness (*dikaiosynē*) which is based on the Law.

10.3: being ignorant of the righteousness (*dikaiosynē*) that comes from God, and seeking to establish their own [righteousness (*dikaiosynē*) is found repeated in some witnesses], they did not submit to God's righteousness (*dikaiosynē*). (4) For Christ is the end of the Law, to bring about righteousness (*dikaiosynē*) for every one who has faith. (5) Moses writes that the one who practises the righteousness (*dikaiosynē*) which is based on the Law shall live by it. But the righteousness (*dikaiosynē*) based on faith says ... .

10.10: one believes with one's heart and so is justified (*dikaiosynē*).

(14.17: the kingdom of God ... [means] righteousness (*dikaiosynē*) and peace and joy in holy spirit.)

It should be immediately apparent that this is an impressive and persistent use of this set of terms; it is proportionately and quantitatively greater than the occurrence of these terms in the letter which shows the next highest occurrence of them, Galatians (*dikaiosynē* 4 times, *dikaioō* 8 times – only the 7 occurrences of this in chapters 2 and 3 can really compare with the frequency of usage in Romans – *dikaios* once, *adikeō* once, and the rest not at all). Why does Paul so concentrate on this group of terms?

In the light of what has been argued in the previous section an obvious answer to this question would be to suggest that in some way righteousness is a controversial topic in Paul's dealings with the Roman Christians. More specifically, it may be suggested that *the accusation had been levelled against Paul's gospel and ministry that they were unrighteous, and that Paul had then to defend himself against this charge by showing that they were in fact righteous.* This would then account for the prominence of 'righteousness' and its cognate terms both in the programmatic 1.16-17 and in the rest of the first eleven chapters.

At first sight this is surprising, for how, one might think, could Paul's gospel and ministry be considered 'unrighteous'? Yet, if one looks at some of the questions posed and answered by Paul in this section of Romans, the suggestion seems anything but far-fetched.

Rom 3.1-8 is a passage that has been the despair of many. Rightly Heikki Räisänen has stressed that it anticipates the problems raised in chapters 9-11.[12] Behind this passage lurks, he argues, a fundamental problem of salvation-history, namely that Paul has in fact broken with, cut loose from, God's covenant made with Israel. Although Paul does not put it thus, the problem is really that the Jews have not rejected Christ because they were unfaithful to the covenant, but rather precisely because they wanted to remain true to it ('Verständnis' 106).

Now this fundamental issue is expressed in terms of the issue of God's righteousness or unrighteousness (3.4-5), God's faithfulness (*pistis*) or unfaithfulness (3.3), or God's truthfulness (*alētheia*) or falsehood (3.4, 7); with some justice S. K. Williams has claimed here that 'the faithfulness of God', 'the righteousness of God' and 'the truthfulness of God' are intended as 'virtual equivalents' by Paul (' "Righteousness" ' 268). What is implied, then, by the raising of this issue is that Paul's gospel has provoked the question whether God has been unfaithful to the chosen people Israel and to the covenant made with them, in short, whether God has behaved unrighteously in the sense that Israel's God has broken faith, and has not kept the promises made to them. As Moxnes observes (*Theology* 56-9), such a view of God's actions, if held by Paul, would be nothing short of blasphemous, treating God as behaving no better than a human being – and not a very moral or upright one at that.

This is then picked up and dealt with more fully in chapters 9-11, where with great emphasis Paul spells out in greater detail in 9.1-5 the answer at which he had hinted in 3.1-2:

> 3.1: What is the Jew's advantage, or what is the benefit of circumcision? (2) A great deal, in every way. In the first place they (the Jews) were entrusted with God's oracles.
>
> 9.1: I speak the truth in Christ, I am not lying, for my conscience bears witness with me in holy spirit. (2) A great pain, a ceaseless agony weighs upon my heart. (3) I could even wish to be accursed (and cut off) from Christ for the sake of my kinsfolk who are related to me by physical descent (literally: according to flesh); (4) for they are Israelites, and to them belong adoption (by God) and glory and covenants and cultic service and promises, (5) to them belong the patriarchs, and from them the Christ comes by physical descent. May the God who is above all be blessed for ever. Amen.

Paul then goes on to argue that the fault does not lie with God, but with unresponsive Israel, even if at times his argument seems to lay the ultimate responsibility for that unresponsiveness at God's door, when he speaks of God's 'hardening' of Pharaoh (9.17-18) or of the possibility of God's creating people as a potter fashions pots, with some of them destined for dishonour or even destruction (9.20-3). But despite that he is insistent that God is not unrighteous (9.14), for God has not rejected the chosen people, Israel (11.1-2), and Israel's eclipse is neither complete (11.1, 25) nor final (11.11, 26, 31); God's ultimate purpose even in seeming judgment and rejection is still one of mercy (11.32). In the meantime God is open to, and ready to receive, all that respond to the divine offer of salvation (10.12-13).

These weighty issues, then, are touched on first in 3.1-8, in response to Paul's line of argument in chapter 2, which is to the effect that the true Jew and the true circumcision are not the outward ones, but the inward and spiritual ones (2.28-9; cf. Phil 3.3);[13] this leads on naturally to the question of the point of being a

Jew or being circumcised in the normal, physical senses of the terms. (And Harder rightly notes that the advantage of these is in fact far from clear – 'Anlaß' 21.) But implicit in that question, as is clear from what follows in vv 2-8, is the issue of whether, if there is indeed no point or advantage in either physical Jewishness or physical circumcision, God has then deluded and deceived Israel in giving them the covenant and promises which they received; for these they understood to be conferring special privileges upon Jewishness and to be assigning a special significance to the rite of circumcision; had God had second thoughts or had they been led astray by the terms of the covenant which they thought that they had received from their God?

However, not only does this passage raise the question of God's righteousness, but in vv 7-8 Paul's argument also leads him on to a further, at first sight unrelated, topic:

> But if through my falsehood God's truthfulness abounded to God's glory, why am I [Paul here speaks in the first person singular for sinful humanity, but in particular, in this context, for sinful Jews] still judged as (being) sinful? (8) And why should we not, as we are falsely accused by some of saying, do evil that good may come of it? These people are justly condemned.

The force of these verses is more clearly articulated in chapter 6, and the problem raised here is more adequately answered than in the somewhat brusque and cavalier response of 3.8. In Romans 6 Paul comes back to what is basically the same objection as that to which he gives expression in 3.7-8: having said in 5.20 that 'where sin abounded, grace abounded all the more', he then in 6.1 raises the question whether Christians ought therefore to persist in sin in order that grace might abound; the abounding of grace is surely something very good, and continued sinning ('doing evil' in the language of 3.8) would give more scope for it. Or, as he puts it in 6.15, are they to sin because they are no longer under the rule of the Law, but under that of grace? Applying this line of thought to 3.7-8, we can then see that Paul is there asking whether, because the falsehood (or unrighteousness) of humanity, and here particularly Jewish humanity, has caused God's truthfulness (or

THE REASONS FOR ROMANS

righteousness) to abound to God's glory, unrighteous people are thereby exonerated from their unrighteousness; more than that, does it imply that they should even continue to be (even more) false or unrighteous so that God's truthfulness and glory might be given further scope and therefore be further enhanced?

It needs to be emphasized at this point that, although Paul may here be using the vivid question and answer style typically found in the popular philosophical lecture or treatise known as the 'diatribe' (see chapter 3 §1 above and n. 2 there), this does not necessarily mean that the questions raised here are purely rhetorical or hypothetical. S. K. Stowers, in his book on *The Diatribe and Paul's Letter to the Romans*, recognizes that sometimes in the writings of Epictetus and Dio of Prusa 'real objections from the audience seem to occur' (128). In his conclusions he seems even more clearly to recognize that this is true in Paul's case too:

> 'objections ... do not simply grow out of the internal logic of the argumentation, but also reflect the teacher's experience of objections and false thinking or behavior which is typical of his audience' (177).

Likewise in this style of writing the conversation partner may be either fictitious or real. In the present case it is reasonably clear from 3.8 that in that case at least Paul is not simply inventing a possible objection to his gospel (one which anyway, it might be argued, does not flow very obviously or naturally from the argument of 3.1-6), but is alluding to, but not yet adequately countering, an objection that really has been levelled against his message. In the light of the argument of this section on God's righteousness in the letter to the Romans it may be thought plausible that the questions raised in 3.1-6 also touch on, and give expression to, issues actually raised by critics of Paul's gospel, and that Paul is therefore answering objections to his message of which the Roman Christians already know or of which Paul fears that they may know or learn.

Thus it is implicit in 3.1-8 that the question of 'God's righteousness' or unrighteousness is linked to the question of the need for those saved to be righteous. In other words, did Paul's message, which, in the eyes of his critics, portrayed God as acting unrighteously, also encourage Christians to act unrighteously as well? That means that 3.1-8 takes up the problem that Paul's gospel apparently denies, as Sanders puts it in his *Paul* (1983) 208, 'two pillars common to all forms of Judaism: the election of Israel and faithfulness to the Mosaic law'; it voices the criticisms that this denial would provoke amongst Jews and Jewish Christians disposed to continue to observe the Jewish Law; this twofold denial would seem to involve a twofold unrighteousness, that of an unfaithful God and that of those encouraged to flout the paths of righteousness laid down in the Mosaic Law.

Now S. K. Williams at one point in his fascinating article on 'The "Righteousness of God" in Romans' seems to want to drive a wedge between the meaning of 'God's righteousness' and plain 'righteousness':

> what Paul says about *dikaiosynē theou* – it is revealed, 'shown up', manifested, demonstrated, and can be known (Rom 1:17; 3:5, 21, 25; 10:3) – he does not say about *dikaiosynē* ; and the kinds of things he says about *dikaiosynē* (cf., e.g., chapter 4; 5:17, 21; 8:10; 9:30; 10:4, 10; 14:17) he does not say about *dikaiosynē theou* (259).

On the other hand if the senses of *dikaiosynē* with and without the qualifying 'of God' are too different, too separated, Paul would be guilty of creating considerable confusion (and perhaps suffering from it himself). It is in fact true that there *does* exist considerable confusion over the meaning of this language in Paul's thought, with the competing claims that '(God's) righteousness' should be regarded as a 'gift', 'power', 'powerful activity' and the like being hotly contested.[14] Is Paul largely responsible for this confusion?

However the differences which Williams notes, and the connections between the seemingly different senses which this term may have, may become more intelligible if we bear in mind that (a) there is rarely a 1:1 equivalence between a Greek term and an English one, and that therefore (b) it is perhaps better to speak of a Greek term as having a 'field of meaning' which may overlap with the 'fields of meaning' of a number of English terms; consequently this 'field' may cover senses that we would have to express by a variety of different English terms, and, because we use different terms for these different senses, it may seem to us that the Greek word is therefore used in different senses. (These points are not peculiar to Greek and English; they are true of more or less any pair of languages. The German 'Uhr' can mean 'hour, time' or 'clock, watch'; the English 'mat' corresponds to one set of German expressions if it is on the floor, to another if it is on a table.) However it may well be that (c) this difference was not so apparent to a native Greek speaker, and that he or she could move from one sense to what seems to us another one without being conscious of doing so.[15]

In the light of this let us consider what Paul says about '(God's) righteousness' in Romans. In some contexts he is quite clearly talking about God's character, and the charge that that character is impugned by his gospel. That is clearly the case, as we have seen, in 3.1-8, and also in 3.25-6: in the latter passage the demonstration of God's righteousness is in order that God may be righteous.

Yet this being righteous is not something that is possible in majestic isolation, for God's 'righteousness' betokens divine action towards someone or something in accordance with this character of 'righteousness'. It is, in other words, essentially a 'relational' and 'practical' term: it is 'relational' in a twofold sense, in that it is (a) measured in relation to certain standards or norms (that which is judged to be 'righteous'), and in that it is (b) exercised in relation to someone or something else. It is 'practical' in the sense that it describes (c) the 'practice', the conduct, the behaviour of someone in relation to someone or something else. In other words someone is 'righteous' when he or she is deemed to be treating someone or something else in a manner that is considered 'righteous'.

Now (a) it may seem odd to describe God as behaving in accordance with certain standards or norms, and at times Paul comes close to implying that this is improper: what right have God's creatures to question what their Creator does with them, any more than a pot can question the actions of the potter that made it (9.20-2). But generally Paul works within the framework of the expectations concerning the conduct of God which had

grown up within Paul's people, Israel, by virtue of their experience of God's dealings with them, although he now seeks to
reinterpret that experience in the light of what he believes to be the
definitive disclosure of God's will and ways, in Jesus Christ. In
other words, it would have been open to him to say, in response to
the charge that his gospel represented God as acting unrighteously
and unjustly, that God was God, and that God's conduct was
therefore beyond human criticism, or at least that criticism was
irrelevant to it; God was above and beyond criticism, and it was
God's prerogative to make the rules, if any, that would govern the
divine activity. However, Paul does not take that course. Instead
he seeks to justify God's ways of dealing with humanity and the
world, as he proclaims it in his gospel, within the framework of the
expectations of the Jews about how God had and would act. He is
concerned that, in the words of Ps 51.4 (50.6 LXX) quoted in 3.4,
God might 'be justified (*dikaioō*) in your words and prevail when
anyone enters into judgment with you'.[16] But Israel's perception
of what was 'righteous' needed to be drastically modified, and
Paul seeks to show that they had not rightly perceived how God
had always acted and therefore were mistaken in their evaluation
of how God would act. Equally, they were therefore mistaken in
their expectations of how God should act and correspondingly of
how God wanted them to respond. So he can turn, for instance, to
God's dealings with Abraham, dealings recognized to be normative and foundational for Israel's self-understanding and its
understanding of its relationship to its God, and try to show how
in fact God dealt in the story of Abraham in a way that was in
keeping with how Paul now proclaimed that same God to be
acting in Christ; the Jews therefore were in error, Paul would
claim, in their interpretation of Abraham's experience of God
(Romans 4).

'Righteousness' is also (b) 'relational' in the sense that it applies
to God's relationships with people and with the world. God, in
other words, could not be 'righteous' except in relation to
someone or something else. 'God's righteousness' is a description
of God's dealings with these other entities. If God alone existed,
and nothing else, if there were only God with nothing or nobody

with which to relate, then the question of the divine 'righteousness' would not arise.

Moreover, (c) this phrase is not just a description of how God views people and the world, but rather it describes God's conduct in relation to those people and that world. It is not just a description of God's being, but also of God's activity.

Now this activity of God does not leave people or the world unaffected; on that Paul and his fellow Jews were agreed. The latter expected the final disclosure of God's righteousness to entail salvation for the faithful and punishment for their enemies; indeed the saving of the former would often be thought to be achieved through the downfall of the latter: the 'salvation' of Israel or the righteous within it was often thought to involve, or to consist in, their being freed from their wicked oppressors. To a certain extent Paul shared that expectation. He too, particularly following the usage of Second Isaiah (Isa 45.8; 46.13; cf. 51.5-6, 8), treated 'righteousness' and 'salvation' as parallel terms (Rom 10.10). Again, the parallelism of Rom 1.17 and 1.18 and the connecting 'for' that links these two verses are best understood if the unexpected present manifestation of God's righteousness has its also paradoxical present counterpart in the revelation of the divine anger. The revelation of God's righteousness that is salvation is no abrogation of the revealed character of Israel's holy God, as if all the standards of that God revealed to Israel had been abrogated; rather it still retains its two-edged quality, both saving and judging at one and the same time. But now, equally unexpectedly for Paul's fellow-Jews, Paul says that this righteousness is an anger or judgment which engulfs all alike, Jew and gentile, for in this matter there is no distinction (cf. 3.9, 20, 22-3). Even the critique which Hellenistic Jews had formulated against the surrounding idolatrous pagan culture (Wis 13-14) is broadened in its application to include the Jews also in Rom 1.18-32; that is implicit in the echoes of Jer 2.5 (*emataiōthēsan* ; and possibly Ps 93.11 LXX, *logismoi , mataioi*) in 1.21, and of Jer 2.11 (*ēllaxato tēn doxan*), Ps 105.19-20 LXX (*ēllaxanto tēn doxan ... en homoiōmati*) and the story of Adam's fall in 1.23.[17] For none of these passages describe the sins of non-Jews, but rather those of Adam, the forefather of all humanity, including the Jews, and of the Israelites who committed the sin of worshipping the golden calf at Mount Horeb, and of the sinful Jews of Jeremiah's day. It is therefore hard to limit the scope of Paul's condemnation in 1.18-32 to non-Jews; all humanity, including the Jews, stand under God's judgment, without excuse before their Creator (1.20, 32).[18] Paul speaks of this judgment being revealed now in the present, as the gospel is preached, and that is perhaps because now the pattern of human rejection of God's gracious approach is shown at its clearest in the turning away from the gospel of Christ; the clearer the manifestation of divine grace, the more glaring the refusal of humanity to respond to it, and in the present instance none are more guilty of that than the Jews who have rejected Christ.

Yet, although the revelation of God's righteousness might entail for Paul, as for his fellow Jews, the revelation of God's wrath, yet it was at the same time for him the revelation that God accepts all humanity on a different basis, that of the saving work of Christ. God justifies all freely, as a gift, by grace (3.24).[19] The term 'justifies' could mean 'declares righteous' or 'makes righteous', and much ink has been expended in the discussion as to whether this 'justification' of which Paul speaks is purely declaratory, or whether it involves an actual 'making righteous'; if it is the latter in what sense are the 'justified' 'righteous'? Put otherwise, is justified humanity simply 'regarded as' righteous (cf. the term 'reckon, account' employed by Paul in Rom 4.3-9; does his use of this commercial term imply that God somehow 'cooks the books', falsifies the records of human sinfulness by treating it as if it did not exist?) or is it really righteous, and, if so, in what sense? However this distinction, while it might work in evaluating the actions of a human ruler or judge, makes no sense applied to the actions of the Creator of all; what the Creator says is the case, is the case and comes into being. Moreover the term 'righteous' is again a relational one: the 'righteousness' that is thus declared, made or created is ultimately a matter of a relationship, of being accepted by, allowed to stand before, God. The distinction between 'declaring' and 'making' is irrelevant: if God declares that one is accepted, one is accepted, at least by God, and after that acceptance, or the lack of it, by any others pales into insignificance.

To be treated thus is, as Paul sees it, something that can properly be compared with being created anew. Thus he takes as an example of Abraham's faith which was reckoned as righteousness Abraham's trust that God would give him descendants; this trust which he had was a trust in a God that makes the dead alive and 'summons things that are not yet in existence as if they already were' (4.17, *NEB*). Then in 4.25, perhaps quoting a traditional Christian formulation, Paul speaks of Christ being handed over to death for our transgressions and being raised for our justification (*dikaiōsis*). The link between Christ's resurrection and our justification here is both unusual (contrast 3.24-5, where the link is, if anything, between Christ's death and our justification) and at the same time most suggestive: the train of thought seems to be that the giving of life to Christ means that that same life is given to all whom Christ represents, and that that sharing in the life given to Christ is described as justification. In other words, so far from being merely a negative act of the not reckoning of sin(s), as might be implied by 4.7-8 taken in isolation, justification is a creative act, calling the justified into a new existence.

One might express this range of meaning, therefore, by saying that justification was seen by Paul as God's putting the world right. It is necessary to recall that 'justify' (*dikaioō*) is a word of the law-courts, and indicates the judge's verdict of acquittal; however in the ancient world this need not be limited to a mere negative verdict that the charge had not been proved against the accused. The role of the ancient judge was a far more positive and creative thing, putting right wrongs in society. *A fortiori* this was seen as true of God as a judge, who is described in Deut 10.18 as one who 'executes justice for the fatherless and widow, and loves the sojourner, giving him or her food and clothing'. God's final act of judgment was, of course, seen by the Jews as also something positive, putting the world to rights and establishing the righteous in the life which had been promised to God's faithful, and at the same time dealing with evil in the world. That intervention by the Judge of all was something which most Jews expected sometime in the future, but now Paul was asserting that that putting right was already happening now, even in the preaching of his gospel (1.16-17), and that it was happening on the basis of grace, rather than of anyone's deserts. So the stress was upon the salvation that God's righteousness, in the sense of God's righteous intervention to put the world right, brought to humanity and the world.

That means that the term 'righteousness (of God)' has a 'field of meaning' that embraces what might seem to us three separate ideas, but ones which might well not have seemed so distinct to Paul and to his readers:

(1) there was that aspect of 'God's righteousness' that related to God's character – the question whether God was 'righteous' or not;

(2) there was the activity of God in which this righteous character of God had to find expression, since 'righteousness' was inconceivable without appropriate activity; the question, therefore, mentioned under (1) above, as to whether God was 'righteous' could only be answered by considering what God had done, as opposed to what God was in abstraction from any activity;

(3) finally there was the state of affairs resulting from that righteous activity, a state of righteousness in human lives and in the world that resulted from God's activity; this aspect is perhaps most clearly seen in another letter of Paul's, in Phil 3.9, where Paul speaks of a righteousness that does not come from (*ek*) (the keeping of) the Jewish Law, but a righteousness that comes from (*ek*), is given by, God.

The theme of 'righteousness' expressed by *dikaiosynē* and its cognate terms has occasioned so much difficulty and argument largely because, I suggest, Paul has in his writings, and particularly in Romans, shifted the focus of his attention around this 'field of meaning' of the term, concentrating now on the question of the character of God, now on the saving activity of God, now on the results of that saving activity, and sometimes even combining more than one of these aspects (as is perhaps the case in 1.17, which, as a programmatic announcement of Paul's theme, should perhaps be interpreted as broadly and as inclusively as possible, with reference to all three aspects). When he drops the qualification 'of God' then it is perhaps most likely to be the third aspect on which he focuses, but that aspect is not to be divorced in thought from the creative activity of God which has brought this state of affairs into being, unless, of course, he is talking of an alternative righteousness that has been established by other means; this is the case, for instance, in Rom 10.3 where the adjective *idios* ('their own') specifies this (cf. Phil 3.9, where he refers to a righteousness that is both his own, and is based on the Law, as opposed to based on God).

What needs to be noted and stressed at this point in the argument of this chapter is that all three aspects of 'God's righteousness' needed to be stressed in Paul's defence of his gospel. It was questioned, firstly, whether the way of life which Paul's gospel called for and encouraged was in fact 'righteous', and therefore whether Paul's ministry could be said to be promoting or furthering 'righteousness' at all (the third aspect above). Secondly, this not only called into question whether this state of affairs could be the product of a God who was regarded as righteous, but, since it involved, it seemed, the setting aside of the covenants and promises made by God with Israel, and the way of 'righteousness' set forth in the Law, it also raised the question whether a God that acted thus could be considered 'righteous' in this respect either; could the actions of this God be characterized as 'righteousness' (the second aspect above)? Therefore, since the actions of God, both in what was created (unrighteous lives, so it seemed) and in what was not done (upholding of the promises and covenants given to Israel) and done (promoting this alternative way that seemed destined to encourage immorality), seemed questionable, the very character of Paul's God was open to question; in other words doubt was cast on the 'righteousness' of Paul's God (the first aspect above). The argument of the main body of Romans in the first eleven chapters has as its main purpose to rebut these charges.

5. The Structure of the Argument of Romans 1-11

It remains to be shown how this defence of Paul's gospel,

announced in the 'I am not ashamed' of 1.16, and the defence of his claim that that gospel indeed discloses 'God's righteousness', is in fact worked out in the argument of the first part of the Letter to the Romans.

One of the most important and suggestive of the many contributions to the study of the purpose of Romans was the article by Nils A. Dahl on 'The Missionary Theology in the Epistle to the Romans'. He saw 1.16-18 as setting out three thematic statements:

(1) The gospel is God's power for salvation, for Jews and for Greeks.

(2) In the gospel God's righteousness is being revealed, 'from faith to faith'.

(3) The wrath of God is revealed from heaven against all ungodliness and wickedness of the human race.

Part of the importance of this is that it does not make a sharp break between 1.17 and 1.18, and thus does justice to the obvious parallelism of structure between these two verses. In fact he binds together 1.15-18 into one unit with the causal statements of the following three verses providing the 'warrant' for the statement of v 15. It is not useful to ask whether vv 16 and 17 are part of the letter opening or 'a short thematic paragraph by itself', for 'in Romans, as elsewhere, the conclusion of one section frequently introduces the theme of the following section' (79). In other words we are wrong always to look for neat, clean breaks in the development of the argument, although there may be some, as we shall see; rather there may well be passages whose function is as a bridge between what precedes and what follows them, with as much claim therefore to be considered part of what preceded as they have to be taken with what follows, and *vice versa*. We need to add, however, in the light of the previous argument of this study, that the present threefold thematic statement needs to be subsumed under Paul's declaration that he is not ashamed of his gospel; in other words he goes on to give a threefold reason for his not being ashamed of it, just as his not being ashamed of it is in turn a, or the, reason for his desire to preach it in Rome (1.15).

How then does Paul develop his argument in **chapters 1-4**? The last two thematic statements about God's righteousness and God's wrath are then, Dahl argues (79, 82), treated in reverse order. In the light of what was said above about the relationship between God's wrath and God's righteousness, these should not, however, be treated as contrasted, but the revelation of God's wrath should be regarded as the revelation of an aspect of God's righteousness; hence the statement of v 18 can be a reason for the statement of v 17: God's righteousness is being revealed, since, for a start, this aspect of it, God's wrath, is being revealed. Moreover, to argue that God's (righteous) wrath and reaction to human sin is being revealed in the preaching of Paul's gospel has added point if Paul's concern throughout this section is to rebut the charge that his gospel makes God out to be unrighteous. The reaction of disobedient humanity to God's self-disclosure, especially the reaction of most Jews to the fullest self-disclosure which has taken place, and is taking place, in the gospel, so far from showing God to be unrighteous, is but evidence of the unrighteousness of those rejecting God's self-disclosure; it has always been God's way to allow those rejecting such a disclosure to go their own way and reap the consequences of their rejection, and it is still so as God is disclosed in Paul's preaching. The Jews in particular will be later charged with not subjecting themselves to God's righteousness (10.3).

The development of the theme of the revelation of God's wrath continues to 3.20 with what Dahl regards as a 'delayed conclusion' in 3.22*b*-23 (ibid.). Again there is therefore no clean break between this section and the following one, but the conclusions of 1.18-3.20 are taken up into the introduction of the following section. This in its turn underlines the close link between God's wrath and God's righteousness. God's way of putting the world right, as Jewish tradition expected it to be manifested, in fact led to a wholly negative and disastrous conclusion: so far from vindicating the Jews and condemning their enemies, it enveloped the Jews too in universal condemnation. The manifestation of God's righteousness, purely on the terms and in the manner that they expected, turned out to be solely a manifestation of wrath. They expected that manifestation to take account of what Paul calls 'works of the Law' (whether he is right in his representation of their expectations is quite another matter),[20] but on that basis 'no living creature will be justified' before God (3.20).

In Paul's development of this theme Dahl rightly notes that 2.6-11 picks up in 2.9-10 the phrase 'the Jew first and the gentile' from 1.16. This Dahl sees as an argument also for questioning those expositions which place a sharp break between 1.32 and 2.1. The rightness of such a break is the more questionable if, as was argued above, Paul already included the sins of Jews under the indictment delivered in 1.18-32. It becomes all the less plausible, then, to argue that 1.18-32 deals with gentiles' sins, and that it is only in 2.1 that Paul turns his attention to the Jews. Indeed Paul's address in 2.1 is quite universal, addressing any and every human being (cf. Schrenk, 'Römerbrief' 90). What is new is that 2.1ff deals with those who pass judgment on their fellows and look down on them from a position of supposed moral superiority, whereas 1.18-32 dealt rather with those who had sinned and those who gave their approval to their sin (1.32), rather than censuring it. One should not assume that Paul believed his fellow Jews to have a monopoly in censoriousness and self-righteousness. It is, after all, only in 2.17 that Paul expressly turns to address his fellow Jews.

2.11 had already introduced a statement about God's impartiality, and 2.17 raises the question of Jewish privilege, a topic which occupies Paul's attention till 3.8. This is intelligible in the light of the apologetic purpose suggested for the whole treatment of God's righteousness: Paul argues that if God's righteousness takes account solely of 'works of the Law' and other 'works' then God will deal equally righteously with all, and that will spell condemnation for the Jew as well as the gentile. God makes no exceptions; to do so would indeed be unrighteous. Therefore Paul's gospel, in abandoning Jewish privilege, does not in so doing abandon God's righteousness, but in fact upholds it. Of course it is one thing to say that God is righteous in the sense of being fair and impartial, but the question of God's being righteous in the sense of being true to those promises that had been given to Israel is another matter. That aspect of God's righteousness, though touched on in 3.1-6, is not dealt with more fully till chapters 9-11.

Having dealt with this question of Jewish privilege to his satisfaction Paul then returns to the theme of God's wrath in 3.9 in order to reiterate his argument that all stand guilty before God, both Jews and gentiles, condemned by the Law (in fact none of the passages quoted here in the catena of Old Testament citations in 3.10-18 are from the Law in the narrower sense of the legal part of the Old Testament; contrast 3.21). That is not to say, of course, that the intervening treatment of Jewish privilege has been a digression, in the sense of a topic that Paul could just as well have omitted from his argument; rather this topic focuses on the issue which has necessitated the treatment of the topic of God's wrath in the first place: Paul must show that God's righteousness, so far from securing the Jew a privileged place secure from God's wrath, in fact demands that that wrath falls upon the Jew no less than the gentile, and perhaps all the more because of Jewish claims to superior knowledge of the way that humanity should walk before their God (cf., e.g., 2.17-21).

The Jews had misread the Law, for the truly saving, rather than entirely condemnatory, revelation of God's righteousness, that which has now taken place in Christ, was attested by that Law and by the prophets (3.21). The relation between this righteousness and God's wrath might be made clearer here by looking ahead to chapter 11 (in itself this underlines how much the first eleven chapters should be regarded as one unit); for there Paul concludes in 11.32 with the assertion that God had shut all people up in *apeitheia*, in an unbelieving and disobedient rejection of the divine revelation, especially, but perhaps not only, the revelation in Christ; this was in order to show mercy on all. He has in 1.18ff described this shutting up of all in disobedience; he now describes how God's righteousness has been made available to all on the basis of grace. Thus Paul returns to the middle of the three themes announced in 1.16-18, the revelation of God's righteousness, to show how it is truly powerful to save as he announced in 1.16. This saving righteousness is, however, exercised through a judgment that leaves all in a state of condemnation for their rejection of the revealed will of God. God judges all in order to save all on the basis of grace.

But again the concerns of Paul's Jewish critics are never far from his mind. Their confidence ('boasting') in the 'Law of works' (i.e. the Jewish Law seen as demanding 'works') is misplaced; God has replaced it by the 'law of faith', i.e. faith as a replacement for the Law (Paul here plays on the word 'law').[21] God has moreover replaced it for all, Jews and gentiles alike (3.28-30).

Then, Paul asks, are we saying that the Law is invalid (3.31)? Here he picks up a charge which in all likelihood his critics levelled against him, although the question and answer style of the passage is again that of the 'diatribe' (Stowers, *Diatribe* esp. 164-7).[22] It may well be that this is to be regarded as a form of instruction, as Stowers argues, in which the questions of a student lead to the teacher's answers, rather than as a confrontation between two opponents. Yet that should not blind us to the fact that Paul's Roman 'students' had, in many cases, ears attuned to the objections of Paul's critics. Paul addresses them as those disposed to learn from him, it is true; that is both polite and diplomatic, it is sound tactics. At the same time it is only realistic to expect that that learning has to take the form of reassurance that those dreadful things are untrue which they have heard, or at least may well hear, about Paul. In other words, these questions are not simply posed for the sake of advancing Paul's argument, but are, yet again, echoes of actual objections that Paul knows have been levelled at his message.

Paul's answer to this particular question has surprised some:[23] not at all, we establish, confirm the Law. It is perhaps, however, not so surprising in the light of Paul's claim that the revelation of God's righteousness was attested by the Law and the prophets (3.21). The trouble here is that Paul speaks of 'the Law' without differentiation, never expressly distinguishing between one part or aspect of it and another, between a valid part of it and an invalid, between a right view and a right use of it and false ones. The aspects of the Law that encourage one to expect salvation from one's 'works' (cf. 'the Law of works' of 3.27) may be different from those that bear witness to the true revelation of God's righteousness in Christ, but Paul never specifies this; both are for him simply 'the Law'. 3.21 thus juxtaposes both elements, both aspects, as starkly and paradoxically as possible: 'apart from the Law ... attested by the Law ...'. Räisänen plausibly sees this tension as rooted in a fundamental tension in Paul's own thought and experience: on the one hand the Law was for him something God-given and holy, but on the other he had grown alienated from the observance of the Law by his years of service in the Law-free mission to the gentiles; Paul is therefore 'torn in two directions, and he is incapable of resolving the tension in terms of theological thought' (*Paul* 264).

Not only is the revelation of God's righteousness attested by the Law, but the principle of justification by faith, by God's grace rather than according to one's deserts, is attested by the Law too, in the case of the patriarch Abraham, the archetypal Jew; for that was the basis upon which he was counted righteous before God (chapter 4). Abraham, for Paul, was far from being what the Jews thought him to be, an example of a Jew faithful to the Law who submitted to circumcision and thus achieved righteousness; for Jews he was also a model for the proselyte, that is for the non-Jew who, like Abraham, entered into God's covenant by submitting to the rite of circumcision and to the Law. Rather, Paul argues, Abraham establishes a pattern for all people by being one who found God's righteousness already outside of, and before, the covenant sealed by circumcision. So far from pointing all who would be part of God's people in the direction of entry into the ranks of Israel through circumcision and obedience to the Law, Abraham, rightly understood (at least by Paul; the view of his Jewish contemporaries, and some Jewish Christians like the writer of the Letter of James, was different), leads all, Jews and gentiles, into independence of, and freedom from, the need for that obedience to the Law that is marked by circumcision; he shows that one can have God's righteousness without obedience of that sort. Abraham's faith is a trust in a life-giving God who can create anew, out of nothing, for that God brought a plentiful lineage and posterity out of Abraham's 'dead' body and Sarah's 'dead' womb (4.19). All can therefore look with a like trust to the God who has already raised Jesus to life as the archetypal pattern and first-fruits of our resurrection and of our 'justification' (4.25).

At the start of chapter 5 Paul quite clearly provides a summary of what has gone before: 'we, having been justified by faith' ('we have received righteousness on the basis of faith') ...'. Most therefore rightly regard this point as the start of a new stage in Paul's argument. But what is this new stage, and what does Paul seek to show in it?

Nygren argued that the structure of the argument of the first eight chapters of Romans was supplied by the quotation from Habakkuk 2.4 in 1.17: 1.18-4.25 were an exposition of the words 'the one who is righteous on the basis of faith', and chapters 5-8 expound the single word translated 'shall live' (*Röm* esp. 30, 36-7; cf. Cranfield, *Rom* 1, 102). Now it is true that, as Nygren pointed out (69), the language of righteous(ness)' and 'faith' is far more prominent in the first four chapters than in 5-8, and the language of 'life' and 'living' is hardly found at all in 1.18-4.25, but far more frequently in 5-8. However it needs to be asked whether it is not rather artificial to find the theme that holds that latter four chapters together in the single phrase 'shall live'. Again, Nygren proposes (33-7) that chapters 9-11 are a treatment of the theme, 'righteousness by faith does not contradict God's promises'; that does not derive from the Habakkuk quotation, so that this proposal raises the question whether chapters 9-11 are to be divorced from chapters 1-8 with 9.1 marking a completely fresh start; or does 5-8 form a digression or interlude before Paul returns to his proper theme of Paul's righteousness, perhaps having been lured on a rather long detour by his exegesis of the Habakkuk text. Neither possibility seems altogether satisfactory.

Equally the traditional division of the first eight chapters between the themes of 'justification' (1-5) and 'sanctification' (6-8) is hardly satisfactory either; for a start it is far more convincing to place the beginning of a new stage in Paul's argument at 5.1 with its summary of the preceding argument. That is not, of course, to overlook the ties that bind chapter 5 to what precedes it; however, to take 5.1-11 or even 5.1-21 with the preceding section (see, for instance, Wilckens, *Röm* 1, 17, 181-2,

286-8, 307) does not seem to do justice to the way in which 5.1 signals that a stage in the argument has been completed in a way that neither 5.12 nor 6.1 does; what may have encouraged this interpretation is the way in which the results of the preceding stage of the argument have been incorporated into the next stage (as was the case also with 3.22*b*-23 in 3.21ff).

Again it is Dahl who proposes an illuminating way to understand the structure of Paul's thought in **chapters 5-8**. In particular he suggests that

(a) Romans 8 contains a restatement of several ideas that are found in 5.1-11 (this is illustrated by a synopsis in an appendix on pp. 88-9).

(b) Paul's argument advances by means of a series of 'theses that are then elaborated or give rise to questions': 5.9-11 with 5.12ff; 5.20-1 with 6.1ff; 6.14 with 6.15ff; 7.5-6 with 7.7ff; (?7.25*a* with 8.1ff;) 8.17*b* with 8.18ff (ibid. 82-3).

(c) The units introduced by the questions in 6.1, 15; 7.7, 13 are best regarded 'as refutations of objections against Paul's doctrine and thus as integral parts of his argumentation' (83).

Chapters 5-8 are, on this view, best regarded as a sort of 'ring-composition', on a grander scale than the examples which we earlier considered in Romans 12 and 13 (chapter 4 §3), although Dahl does not here use this term. (However Peter von der Osten-Sacken, who largely follows Dahl here, does: *Römer 8* 60.) Chapter 8 picks up and restates more fully a number of ideas broached in 5.1-11 and indeed provides an essential commentary on, and supplement to, the earlier and briefer statement of these ideas in that chapter:

Apart from the climactic chain in Rom. 5:3-4 and the aside in Rom. 5:7, all major themes in Rom. 5:1-11 reappear in Romans 8: Justification and a restored relationship to God as the basis for the hope of future salvation and glory in spite of present sufferings; the gift of the Holy Spirit, the death of Christ, and the love of God as warrants for this hope; a note of exultation (ibid. 89).

Dahl goes on to note that 5.1-11 differs from chapter 8 partly by being 'closely linked' to chapters 1-4, whose argument it brings to a 'preliminary conclusion'; he points to the references to 'by faith' and 'grace' in 5.1-2, Christ's death for the ungodly while we were still helpless and sinners and enemies (5.6-10), and the mention of salvation 'by his blood' and 'from the wrath' in 5.9. Some of these (the references which he cites in 5.1-2 and 9 especially) are recognizably recapitulating ideas from chapter 8; our being weak and our having been God's enemies are more readily paralleled in Rom 8.26 and 8.7-8 respectively (surprisingly Dahl's synopsis mentions neither of these).

Moreover, if the argument earlier (in §3 above) is sound then, as we have seen, 5.1-11 picks up another theme which links up with the affirmation in 1.16 that Paul is not ashamed of his gospel: Paul gives vent to an expression of his confidence in his gospel and of the hope engendered by it, and that is the theme which runs through chapters 5-8, rounded off by the ringing and lyrical declaration of confidence contained in 8.31-9. Hope and confidence are, however, particularly prominent in chapters 5 and 8, but far less so in 6 and 7.

Even 5.12-21 is less obviously a treatment of this theme than 5:1-11. Dahl's explanation of this passage is that

> the analogy between Adam and Christ in 5:12-19 illuminates and supports the main thesis in 5:1-11, that justification is a sure ground for the hope of final salvation and life. (ibid. 82)

In particular it is, as he suggests slightly later, the declaration of 5.9-11 that triggers off this elaboration. Certainly these verses are linked with 5.12ff by the formal similarity of the arguments from the lesser to the greater found in vv 9-10 and in 15 and 17 ('... how much more ...') as well as by the repeated theme of the 'abounding' of grace found in vv 15, 17 and 20 which could be regarded as making the same point in a different form and language. At the same time it is to be noted that 5.12-21 is introduced, not by a causal conjunction, but by a 'therefore'. It should accordingly be seen as taking Paul's argument a stage further: the certainty of grace and the salvation (5.9-10) and reconciliation with God (5.11) that this grace has brought leads Paul on to a further conclusion, that the obedience of this one human being, Christ, has more than counteracted the baneful effects of the disobedience of our common human ancestor, Adam. This is, in its turn, a further ground for confidence in redemption from that futility to which creation was subjected according to 8.20-1, in all probability an allusion to the curse of Gen 3.14-19 that followed upon Adam's disobedience.

Yet at the same time that raises the question why the exposition of chapter 8 is delayed by the inclusion of 6.1-7.25. The contents of these chapters are certainly hard to describe as furthering Paul's argument that his gospel was one of hope and that it would disappoint neither its preacher nor those that trusted in it. Again, however, there is much to be said for the explanation offered by Dahl, that Paul here deals with objections to his gospel.

In one sense these objections can be said to be triggered by things that Paul says in the course of the argument of Romans. Thus, as we saw, Dahl considers that 6.1-14 is triggered by 5.20-1, 6.15-7.6 by 6.14, 7.7-12 by 7.5-6, and 7.13-25 by 7.12. Paul's language bears this out in some measure: the question of 6.1, whether we should continue to sin so that grace might abound (*pleonazō*) picks up the language of 5.20, although *pleonazō* is there used of transgression or sin's abounding and another term, *hyperperisseuō*, is used of grace's 'abounding even more'. 6.15 picks up the idea of our being 'not under law but under grace' found in 6.14 and asks whether this means that we should sin.

With 7.7-25, however, the verbal signals are not so clear, and with this passage, and indeed with 6.1-7.6 too, we are better to look beyond the mere words used to the content of the passages that precede each of these passages. In 5.20 not only do we find the idea that sin's abounding is matched by a superabundance of grace, which provokes the suggestion that the Christian is best to go on sinning, but we also find before it in the first part of the verse the idea that the coming of the Law occasioned the abounding of transgression. Objections arising from these two ideas are then dealt with in reverse order:

(1) the abundance of sin leading to the superabundance of grace and the consequent suggestion that we should foster and encourage grace by causing sin to abound still further is answered in three stages in 6.1-7.6. In (a) 6.1-14 this is dealt with by stating that we

have died with Christ to sin, in (b) 6.15-23 by the idea that one must choose between two masters, sin and death on the one hand or righteousness and God on the other, and in (c) 7.1-6 by the analogy of a husband's death freeing a wife to marry another husband; death with Christ to the Law (and its attendant sins) sets us free to belong to and serve Christ.

(2) 7.7-25 then deals with the problematic suggestion that the Law's coming produced transgression, and at the same time picks up the question that might well have been provoked by the reference in 7.5 to the 'passions of sins which arise through the Law' that were at work in our bodies so as to produce a harvest for death. Both of these remarks lead to the question whether the Law is sin, a question which Paul seeks to answer in 7.7-25.

However the arguments of these two chapters do not deal with questions that arise only out of what Paul has just said in writing to the Romans. They are likely also to be answers to real objections raised against Paul by his critics. For we have already seen that 3.8 anticipates the problem broached in 6.1, and 3.8 clearly suggests that Paul is here not just propounding an imaginary or theoretical objection to his gospel, but is echoing something which others have actually said about it. 3.31 too, it was suggested, echoed a charge against Paul, that he was discarding the Law. 7.7 faces a graver version of the same line of criticism, the charge that Paul was vilifying the God-given Law by making it out to be something sinful. It is not hard to believe that that too was a complaint actually levelled against Paul by his critics.

Both of these lines of criticism, that Paul's gospel encouraged sin, and that it denigrated the Law, were adequate reasons for Paul's critics to claim that his gospel was something shameful, and something that impugned God's righteousness. (And interestingly Paul says that converts' former life, in which his critics were suggesting that he was saying they should continue, was one of which they are now ashamed: *epaischynomai*, 6.21; by implication their life would be shameful if they continued in these ways as it was suggested that Paul was encouraging them to do.) By the arguments of 6.1-7.25 Paul rebuts these charges, as indeed he must if he is to show that the preaching of his gospel is indeed a revelation of God's righteousness and if he is thus going to be able to insist that it is nothing shameful.

Nor does it put him to shame in the sense of causing him or itself to be found wanting. To that theme, started in chapter 5, but temporarily, yet necessarily, interrupted, Paul returns in chapter 8, as he picks up the subject of the reasons for his hope and confidence in the message which he proclaims, but speaks of them, as Dahl notes (ibid. 85), in the light of what he has just said about human bondage to sin and death in 7.7-25. Worthy of note, too, is Luz's suggestion ('Aufbau' 166) that, while 7.5 sets the theme of 7.7-25, 7.6 with its reference to a service in newness of spirit heralds the subject-matter of chapter 8. So he speaks of the life and freedom engendered by the outpouring of God's spirit, announced already in 5.5, of the service of, and obedience to, the spirit, and of the adoption which the possession of that spirit attests, and of the consequent status of fellow-heirs with Christ. Strikingly, however, he speaks, as we saw in the previous chapter (§3), of the possession of the spirit enabling those controlled by it to fulfil the 'just requirement' (*dikaiōma*) of the Law (8.4), a stark rebuttal of the charge that his gospel promoted the abandonment of any morality; not even the morality of the Law was jettisoned, but rather in fact it was now for the first time fulfilled. However in 8.17 he adds on a qualification that those who would share Christ's inheritance in glory must share his sufferings now; that leads Paul on to describe how, if sufferings abound now in creation, these will be more than compensated for in the coming glory that is yet to be revealed, a topic that takes him back to the subject of 'hope' (8.24-5). The chapter, and surely too this entire section of Romans, closes with a triumphant affirmation of the sure confidence (8.38: *pepeismai*, 'I am convinced') which Paul's gospel engenders, for it produces the unshakable conviction that nothing can separate us from God's love in Christ. At the same time Luz argues (ibid. 181; cf. 179) that chapters 6-8 are also very much concerned with how God's righteousness takes on a concrete form. In other words, Paul is not ashamed of his gospel because he is at all points able to show that his gospel does not impugn God's righteousness by promoting unrighteousness

(6.1-7.6) or by suggesting that God has given Israel an unrighteous Law (7.7-13) and that his gospel in fact effects a new, spirit-led righteousness in those who obey it.

9.1 marks a fresh start, a further phase in the argument, with its dramatic shift from the jubilant expectation of salvation at the end of chapter 8 to Paul's heartsearching at the start of chapter 9, provoked perhaps by the sight of an Israel apparently excluded from salvation (cf. Schrenk, 'Römerbrief' 99). We have already seen that the contents of **chapters 9-11** are foreshadowed by 3.1-6: the issue is the righteousness of God's dealings with Israel in the light of the facts that Paul propounded a gospel which offered Israel's heritage to gentiles without the covenant obligation to keep the Jewish Law, and that the Jews had largely rejected that gospel and in Paul's eyes were therefore preventing themselves from entering into and enjoying their heritage.

In this section (9.1-11.36) it becomes clearer that at times Paul needs to carry on his argument on two fronts. For, on the one hand, he defends his gospel by showing that God's dealings in Christ as proclaimed in his gospel have been righteous, and indeed are in continuity with the treatment of Israel down the centuries: it has always been the case that only a few in Israel have remained truly faithful to their God, that only a few have enjoyed the promised covenant relationship with their God. That argument makes sense directed to an audience that included some who were disposed to criticize Paul's gospel for representing God as dealing unrighteously. In this section, though, we also meet again the theme of not being ashamed or put to shame, with its consequent echoes of 1.16: in 9.33 and 10.11 Paul quotes Isa 28.16 to the effect that 'the one who trusts in it (the stone of stumbling and the rock of offence; in 10.11 at least, where the first part of the Old Testament verse is omitted, the pronoun would most easily be taken as referring to Jesus) will not be put to shame (*kataischynomai*)'. Again Paul expresses his confidence in his gospel that proclaims that one will be saved by faith alone; one does not need the misplaced efforts and zeal of the Jews which led them to seek to set up their own righteousness (10.2-3). Again, those who were most likely to level charges of the kind which

Paul's arguments here rebut would be either Jews or Christians of a Judaizing kind who shared Jewish reactions to Paul's message.

On the other hand Paul does explicitly address himself to gentiles in 11.13, and the whole thrust of the following argument is intelligible, not if it is addressed to Judaizing Christians, but if it is an appeal to gentile Christians who are disposed to write off the Jews and their special relationship to God as finished and outdated (so Williams, '"Righteousness"' 252, despite his tendency to follow those who see in Romans the development of 'an argument especially relevant to a defense of his mission in Jerusalem' – ibid. 248). In the light of this we can perhaps detect other traces earlier in the letter of this other 'front' within Paul's argument which is in general directed to his Judaizing critics: in 6.15-23, for instance, Paul seems aware that not only must he satisfy his critics that his gospel does not entail continued sinning, but also that he must show those who have espoused that gospel that they must not go on sinning. This makes sense if there were those who went to greater lengths than Paul would or would wish, not only to cut themselves loose from Israel and Judaism (the problem dealt with in chapter 11), but also to cut themselves loose from any moral restraint or guidance that Israel's Law offered. In other words there were those who saw in freedom from the Law an opportunity for licence, and who needed to be reminded that, although free from the obligations imposed by the Law, they were by no means free from all obligations. It is probably against some such problem as this that, as we saw in chapter 4 §2, Paul contends in 1 Cor 6.12-20: there were those who claimed that all was lawful for them, and thus in particular claimed their right to break with those tabus which Jews felt most to distinguish their morality based on the Law from that of the gentiles around them, namely restraints on sexual behaviour (the problem in 1 Cor 6 – some Christians apparently felt free to enter into a sexual relationship with prostitutes) and contacts with idolatry (the problem in 1 Cor 8-10, where the slogan of 6.12 is echoed in 10.23). The existence of those who interpreted the Law-free gospel thus could only have encouraged the suspicions of Paul's critics and their charge that his gospel promoted immorality or unrighteousness.

Yet by 11.25 Paul no longer seems to have such over-zealous supporters of the Law-free gospel particularly in mind, and it is therefore probably best to see him as here addressing both his critics and those that espoused freedom from the Law and from Judaism, and who wrote Israel off; he shares with both the 'mystery' of God's purposes in the partial hardening of Israel. God's will is for the salvation of all (11.32); God is not unrighteous or unfaithful, for the divine gifts and calling are irrevocable (11.29). What God has given in grace has not been taken back nor been lost for ever, and God's call still sounds forth. God's ways may be hard to discern, but Paul is confident of the ultimate righteousness of God's dealings (11.33-6).

As a result we find a structure in Paul's argument in this main body of his letter to the Romans that can be represented as follows:

1.15: Paul is eager to preach the gospel in Rome,

[A] for he is not ashamed of this gospel, for it is God's power for saving all (1.16),

[B] for in it God's righteousness is being revealed (1.17),

for [C] in it God's wrath is being revealed against all humanity, both Jews and gentiles (1.18-3.20/23).

(2.17-3.8: are the Jews privileged?)

[B] (3.20-4.25) The revelation of God's righteousness. (3.31-4.25: the Law is not abrogated by this message, for it testifies to justification by faith in the case of 'righteous' Abraham.)

[A] 5.1-8.39: Paul's gospel does not put the one who believes to shame.

(6.1-7.6: the Christian should not continue in sin, but has broken with it.

7.7-25: the Law is not sinful.)

[B] 9.1-11.36: God has dealt righteously with Israel, both in the past and in the present, and Israel still has a special place in the divine purposes.

It needs, however, to be stressed again that those sections of the argument that have been placed in brackets in the outline above are not digressions; Paul is not sidetracked in these, but rather focuses in them on those aspects of his argument which most directly bear on the issues which had occasioned that argument in the first place; these issues are the criticisms brought to bear on Paul by his critics, speaking from the viewpoint of a Judaizing version of Christianity.

This chapter has attempted to show that the seemingly very general argument of Romans 1-11 is by no means written without any reference to the situation of the Roman Christians. Rather its main purpose is to answer those criticisms of Paul's gospel and ministry which would prevent the Christians in Rome who had espoused a Judaizing form of Christianity from offering their support, their endorsement and their prayers for the success of his visit to Jerusalem with the collection; the same criticisms and suspicions, if not allayed, would in turn have presented him with considerable difficulties when eventually he reached Rome and sought to exercise his ministry amongst them as their apostle.

At the same time, however, Paul writes with at least half an eye on the attitude of those who had espoused the Law-free gospel in Rome. Their attitude, if carried to extremes, threatened to confirm the worst fears of the Jewish and Judaizing Christian critics of Paul's mission by their licentious behaviour, and at the same time their contempt for, and rejection of, Israel's heritage was likely to render them less than enthusiastic about Paul's collection for the Jerusalem church.

Earlier we also saw how these respective attitudes to the Jewish Law and Jewish traditions were creating tensions within the Roman Christian community; intolerance was ousting loving appreciation of, and concern for, the needs and claims of those holding these two very different views of Christian faith and its relationship to life under the Law. The arguments of chapters 1-11 prepare the ground for the way in which Paul seeks to address this divided community in the appeals which follow in chapters 12-15 (see chapter 4 §3) by allaying the fears and suspicions that fostered these divisions and tensions.

VI

CONCLUSIONS

At the outset of this study it was suggested that it was a mistake to look for just a single reason for Paul's writing his letter to the Romans, so complex was the evidence presented by that letter for which any such explanation had to account. That complex evidence included the relationship between the letter-frame on the one hand, which reflected Paul's actual situation at the time of writing and his relations with the Roman church, and the main body of the letter on the other, which seemed at first sight so divorced from any actual set of circumstances. Then there was not only Paul's situation, but also that of the Roman Christians; did that not have to be brought into the reckoning if we were to understand the letter, or was Romans in this respect unlike any other Pauline letter, unrelated to any actual situation or needs of the recipients? But in that case why did he write precisely this letter, and why did he write it to them in particular? Finally there is the conflicting evidence in the letter as to the nature of the audience to whom Paul addressed himself in writing: were they Jews, Jewish Christians, gentile Christians or what?

To take the last question first: we have seen how Paul in fact has to address an audience that is divided, and divided along a line marked out by the conflicting attitudes of those in it towards Paul's Law-free mission to the gentiles. Some welcomed that message, but tended to push its logic further than Paul desired and in directions unwelcome to him; they sought to sever their ties with Israel and things Jewish. But there were others in the Roman church whose attitude was very different; the church there had in all likelihood been established initially along very Jewish lines, and had adopted a form of Christianity which embraced many of the practices of Judaism and remained in contact with the synagogue. Despite the disciplinary measures of Claudius this Christian tradition had remained in Rome and was perhaps increasing again in strength as the years passed after that emperor's death. To those who remained in this tradition, and they by no means need have been confined to those who were Jews by birth, Paul's gospel and ministry, like the conduct of those following such a gospel in Rome, were an object of grave suspicion. They shared much of the misgivings, outrage even, of non-Christian Jews both at the seeming blasphemy of Paul's account of the story of God's dealings with Israel and the world and at the actual or threatened immorality of his converts. These two groups of Christians were divided amongst themselves over their observance or non-observance of the Jewish Law.

Thus the Roman Christians on the one hand needed, some of them, to appreciate the Jewishness of the Christian tradition; on the other hand others of them needed to see how Paul's gospel proclaimed a God who was acting now in a way consistent with the Old Testament's record of how God had always acted in dealing with Israel, and also to understand that Christians were ushered into a new and better service of their God that was still moulded by the righteousness of their Lord. The main thrust of Paul's argument in the body of the letter is thus to maintain that the preaching of his gospel does reveal God's righteousness, which his Judaizing critics doubted. At the same time the followers of the Law-free gospel needed to be reminded both that that gospel does still call for righteousness, and that they could not shake themselves loose from the Jewishness of the faith which they had received.

These arguments needed to be presented to the Roman Christians at that point of time both because Paul wanted their support and backing for his journey to Jerusalem with the collection, and because Paul, setting his sights on future work, saw the time drawing near for the realization of his long-held hopes to extend his work to the West. There was a church at Rome, a gentile church; it was therefore in principle one of his churches, for which he was responsible, and which was responsible to him. It should support him in the venture that lay before him in the immediate future; it should also welcome him when eventually he came to it. His fear was that it would be united in doing neither of these, for the issue of support for the collection brought to a head the divisions and tensions already existing within the Roman Christian community, and the arrival of Paul himself in person could only exacerbate that situation yet more, unless the misunderstandings and misapprehensions of his message could be corrected. So he hoped by writing now both to secure support for the Jerusalem visit and at the same time to prepare the way and ease the path for his future visit to Rome.

The reasons for Romans are thus a cluster of different interlocking factors: the presence of both Judaizing and Law-free Christians in the church there, the present situation of the church in Rome and the present situation of Paul, the visit to Jerusalem now being undertaken and the prospect of a future visit to Rome. All played their part in provoking Paul to write to the Roman Christians as he did, and the Christian church in succeeding centuries is much the richer because he did.

NOTES

Notes on chapter 1

[1] Cf. also the surveys in Campbell, 'Debate', 'Paul' and 'Romans III'; Drane, 'Paul'; Kettunen, *Abfassungszweck* 7-23; cf. also Wedderburn, 'Purpose'; Zeller, *Juden* 38-44 and *Röm* 15 (short bibliography), etc.

[2] D. Nineham in *SJTh* 29 (1976), 291.

[3] Artemon in [Demetrius of Phalerum], *On Style* §223; cf. White, *Light* 190-1.

[4] In his *Loci communes* of 1521 (ed. Engelland 2.1, 7).

[5] Cf. further examples in Beker, *Paul* 69 (Bruce, *Paul* 326 – endorsing Lightfoot – and Keck, *Paul* 15-16); also Kettunen, *Abfassungszweck* 7 n.1.

[6] Cf., e.g., Stowers, *Letter Writing* ; White, *Light*.

[7] *Theologische Studien und Kritiken* (1829) 609ff cited in Kümmel, *Introduction*[2] 318 n. 45.

[8] Cf. Wedderburn, 'Chronologies' 107.

[9] Cf. the use of the epithet *Narcissianus* in *CIL* 3.3973; 6.9035, 15640.

[10] Cf. the bibliography given in Kettunen, *Abfassungszweck* 17 nn. 1, 4.

Notes on Chapter 2

[1] 'Sweeping round' is one rendering of the adverb used here, the one preferred by BAG 458*a* and most comms; 'and its environs' was suggested by B. Weiß, but has found little favour. Acts

records no activity of Paul in Illyricum; some have tried nevertheless to find room for work there.

2 The alternative is to see this as a reference to a *praetorium* , the residence of a provincial governor; the advantage of the rendering given above is that it enables this word to be given a personal sense analogous to that of the following 'all the others'.

3 But for Lüdemann, *Christentum* 233, this list cannot be of those accompanying Paul with the collection, for delegates from Corinth and Philippi are not mentioned; rather these are those who assisted Paul in missionary work in the area of Troas. But are we sure that Corinth eventually participated or that a delegate from Philippi is not included in the 1st person plural?

4 This somewhat unfashionable qualification is included because of the tension between two factors: (1) the observation that it is hard to explain why Acts ends when it does unless some version of the text were written at the end of Paul's two years of imprisonment at Rome and before any further developments were known; (2) the awareness that Acts in its present form presupposes the existence of the third Gospel in some form or other (Acts 1.1) and most date Luke in its present form (I leave aside the equally unfashionable, but not therefore necessarily erroneous, theory of a 'Proto-Luke') considerably later than the early 60's when Paul was probably imprisoned. As yet I have found no altogether satisfactory way to reconcile these two factors. The possibility that there was an earlier edition of Acts I add in the face of the insistence of some that the style of the 'we'-passages is indistinguishable from that of the rest of Acts (cf. Haenchen, *Apostelgeschichte* 93: 'We can detect no sources in Acts from differences in style'), but that of course does not rule out the possibility, even likelihood, that the author has used sources, but has assimilated them to his or her own style.

5 An identification of the two Gaii is perhaps the likeliest explanation of the Western reading followed by the *NEB*, 'Gaius the Doberian' (making him come from a Macedonian town); cf. the discussion in Metzger, *Commentary* 475-6.

6 Cf. the discussion of the evidence in Theißen, *Setting* 75-83.

7 Kettunen also advances the interesting suggestion that the 'therefore' at the start of 15.22 is there because the existence of the Roman church made his coming superfluous (*Abfassungszweck* 136; cf. Suhl, Anlaß' 129). But is it not odd, and surprisingly negative, to speak of the existence of a church there 'hindering' his coming to them? This interpretation would only work if 'therefore' means 'therefore (I wanted to come to you too, but) I was also many times prevented ...' (this theory has only accounted for one time). Cf. further in chap. 5 n. 7. Suhl makes the further suggestion that Paul had been on his way to Rome on the Via Egnatia, through Illyricum, when news of Claudius' expulsion of the Jews in 49 made him aware of the existence of Christians already in Rome; I think it likelier that it would have deterred him from a visit because as a Jew himself he would hardly have found this the most opportune time for a visit.

8 On the problematic syntax of these verses cf. Cranfield ad loc.

9 Cf. Add. Esth. to 4.17 (14.17 in *RSV*); this passage suggests an aversion to wine because of its use in pagan libations (cf. Watson, *Paul* 95).

10 Cf. also Hecataeus quoted in Jos., *Ap.* 1.199.

11 Various versions of this work are to be found: K. H. Kuhn's translation in Sparks, *Apocryphal Old Testament*, has no exact equivalent but cf. his 5.6; also Rießler, *Schrifttum* 1139 – his 4.8.

12 Cf. Schürer, *History* 1, 460.

13 Cf., e.g., Wilckens, *Röm* 3, 114 at nn. 553-6: Eus., *Hist. eccl.* 2.23.5; Epiph., *Haer.* 30.15.3; Hipp., *Ref.* 7.28.7; 8.20.1.

14 I find this more plausible than the suggestion of Watson, *Paul* 95, that Jews returning after Claudius' expulsion found themselves unable to resettle in the Jewish quarter and were therefore unable to obtain ceremonially pure meat and wine; for a start it is not clear whether by the time of Claudius' expulsion the Jews were still confined to a specific quarter (the Trastevere – Schürer, *History* 3.1, 75) since they 'gradually ... spread through the city' (ibid. 79); nor would residence in another quarter render it impossible to obtain ritually pure commodities (and frequent eating of meat was more characteristic of higher

social classes, who would be likely to have servants to send to obtain it – Theißen, *Setting* 125-8). If one were to seek an explanation along these lines it might be more plausible to postulate that Claudius' expulsion had dislocated the source of supply of these commodities by expelling the suppliers; but probably they too would have returned by now.

15 On the collection cf. Georgi, *Geschichte* ; Nickle, *Collection*.

16 Cf. Jewett, *Dating* ; Knox, *Chapters* ; Lüdemann, *Paulus* 1; cf. Wedderburn, 'Chronologies'.

17 If the 'famine relief visit' of Acts 11.30 is in fact the occasion of this Jerusalem agreement (as seems likely – cf. Wedderburn, ibid. 107) then this translation of the present subjunctive, 'continue to remember', seems more appropriate.

18 On the view that Gal 2.7 contains (at least some of) the wording of the Jerusalem agreement, including its implicit recognition of the existence of two different gospels (despite 1.7), as well as the use of the name Peter as opposed to Paul's more usual Cephas and the ascription of apostleship to Peter but not to Paul, cf. Betz, *Gal* ad loc.

19 However it seems unlikely that Gal can be as early as some English-speaking scholars wish to date it – perhaps even the earliest of Paul's extant letters (e.g. Bruce, *Gal* 55) – for it seems unlikely that Paul could properly address the churches in Pisidia and Lycaonia founded on his first missionary journey as 'Galatians'.

20 On the different opinions of Jewish Christians on this matter cf. R. E. Brown in Brown–Meier, *Antioch* 2-8.

21 I am grateful to Professor E. Best for the observation that, for whatever reasons, Paul never seems to mention troubles with any of his churches when writing to another church. (However Phil 1.15-17 might be an exception to this.)

Notes on Chapter 3

1 Jos., *Bell.* 2.119=*Ant.* 18.11 (cf. *Vita* 11) witnesses to some of the diversity within Palestinian Judaism, listing the three movements of the Pharisees, the Sadducees and the Essenes; Philo,

Migr. Abr. 89-90 points to the different approaches to the question of the literal observance of the Law in Judaism.

[2]See the summary by E. G. Schmidt in *Der kleine Pauly* 2 (1975) 1577-8: 'The whole concept [of the diatribe] has again and again been questioned. On the one hand the most common description of the diatribe as 'Cynic-Stoic' was found to be too narrow; even Bion [of Borysthenes, 3rd cent. B.C.E., credited with being the pioneer of this literary form] was not really a Cynic, and later literature from quite different schools also used the form of the diatribe. On the other hand the stylistic differences between the *spoudogeloion* [a blend of levity and seriousness] of the Hellenistic diatribe and the at once more serious and more more austere didactic writings of the imperial period (e.g. Musonius) cannot be overlooked.' Yet 'to describe certain characteristics of style and thematic patterns in ancient popular philosophical literature the concept of the diatribe ... is doubtless useful, although it should not be used in the sense of a closely defined genre and should not be applied too widely.' See further Stowers, *Diatribe*, especially chapter 1, and most recently Schmeller, *Paulus*, which appeared too late to be used in this study to any great extent.

[3] Watson, *Paul* 97, speaks of 'two congregations' in Rome, but (1) there may have been more than just two, and (2) as mentioned below Paul could address divided churches as one; however in this case the differences would involve the question of table-fellowship between those faithful to the Law and those who did not keep it, and this would have made it difficult for some to meet with others.

[4] But see the hesitancy of Bruce, *Heb* 254-5 on this point.

[5] Although Heb 2.3 *need* not imply that the author was any further removed from the founding events of the Christian faith than Paul himself was, 13.7 suggests, however, a time when the founders of the church no longer lived.

[6] Cf. Räisänen, '"Hellenists"' 266, who also questions the accuracy of the future tense here.

Notes on Chapter 4

[1] Examples of this and similar constructions can be found in most of the Pauline letters; from the *homologoumena* Bjerkelund also lists 1 Cor 1.10; 4.16; 16.15-16; 2 Cor 10.1-2; 1 Thess 4.10-12; 5.14 as primary examples, and as related constructions 2 Cor 2.8; 6.1; Gal 4.12 (using *deomai*); Phil 4.2-3; 1 Thess 4.1; 5.12-13, 27; Philemon 9-12.

[2] See *Ant.* 5.97, 110; 8.52; 12.279; 13.45, 48.

[3] It is perhaps worth noting that much of the thinking about the 'remnant' which Paul employs in his argument in Rom 9-11 (esp. 9.27-9; 11.1-7, 25) may reflect the self-understanding of these Judaizing Christians at Rome. He would then be using their own ideas to answer their criticisms of his gospel as well as to lead gentile Christians to a proper appreciation of Israel's place in God's purpose and of their own debt to them.

[4] Cf. Schürer, *History* 2, 270-2; cf. Jos., *Ant.* 18.312-13.

[5] Cf. Cranfield, *Rom* (ICC) ad loc.

[6] Friedrich-Pöhlmann-Stuhlmacher, 'Situation' 150, argue that 12.3-16a form one self-contained section, followed by another, 12.16*b*-13.7, dealing with 'doing the good' (cf. 12.2) in the form of living with peace with all people. Here I would argue that 12.16*b* goes better with 16*a* rather than as an introduction to 12.17ff, with which it has relatively little in common.

[7] Cf. 1 Cor 14.3, 5, 12, 26, and the cognate verb *oikodomeō* in 8.1, 10; 10.23; 14.4, 17; cf. 1 Thess 5.11.

[8] Jülicher and Lietzmann cited by Käsemann, *Röm* 366.

[9] At least in Paul's case these accusations were unwarranted; in the case of some of his followers, some of his Corinthian converts for instance (cf., e.g., 1 Cor 5.1-8; 6.12-20), who perhaps took freedom from the Law further than Paul himself the accusations may not have been wholly unfounded.

[10] Some MSS read 'welcomed us' instead of 'welcomed you'. Metzger, *Commentary* 536, supports the latter reading by arguing that it has 'superior and more diversified support', which is true in some measure, and that it is 'in harmony with the other instances of the second person plural in the context (verses 5-7)'; the latter seems to me to be a reason for

considering the first person plural to be the more difficult reading and thus the one more likely to be changed by a copyist. Whichever is correct, however, Paul means that Christ has accepted a body of people that includes both Jews and gentiles, and that is true whether the body of people is solely the Roman church ('you') or a wider one.

Notes on Chapter 5

1 Colossians is also written to a church that Paul neither founded nor had visited (2.1); whether or not Paul himself wrote it is disputed (in many respects it is easier to regard it as the work of another's hand), but its opening greeting is far shorter; that may be because the church there was founded by one of Paul's colleagues, Epaphras (1.7), and so, unlike the Roman Christians, could be assumed to be familiar with what Paul stood for and to be within his sphere of authority.

2 Cf., e.g., Dunn, *Unity* 241f; Klijn–Reinink, *Evidence*, e.g. Index s.v. Baptism of Jesus; Birth of Jesus, natural.

3 See further above chap. 2 §1 and n. and also below at n. 7.

4 Amongst others Fiorenza, 'Situation', urges that we should not be deluded or mesmerized by Paul's rhetoric into accepting his perspective on any particular situation as the only possible one or necessarily the correct one.

5 Kettunen interestingly argues against giving a material sense to the being sent to Spain with their 'support' (*NEB*) which is mentioned in 15.24 – it was the way of Paul's opponents to seek that sort of support. Rather it was that they should approve of his mission there, for Spain was a 'Roman field [of operations?]' (could this not be said with equal justice of many parts of the Roman Empire?) – *Abfassungszweck* 167-9.

6 His point would be borne out by texts like 2 Cor 1.8; Gal 1.11; Phil 1.12; 1 Thess 2.1.

7 Kettunen (*Abfassungszweck* 118, 125-38) argues that Paul is referring to a desire that he had had before a church had been established at Rome, i.e. he had desired to be the first to preach there and to found a church there. This seems to me open to

question; for a start was Paul active as a Christian missionary before a church was founded in Rome, let alone aware that he had a particular and special responsibility for the gentile world? Our knowledge of the beginnings of Christianity at Rome are too scanty, even almost non-existent, to allow of certainty here. Moreover Kettunen's proposal involves him in arguing that Paul's coming to Rome to evangelize had been made superfluous now by the founding of the church there. If that implies that 1.15 refers only to the past it is surely difficult to supply a past tense of the verb 'to be' after the present 'I am' in 1.14? (See also chap. 2 §1 and n. 7.)

8 It would seem that the term 'gospel' (*euangelion*) can mean for Paul both the activity of preaching and what is proclaimed; in 1.1 it makes better sense to take this word in the former sense, but in the present context both senses may be present.

9 In recent years, particularly among North American scholars, the still prevailing consensus that this phrase contained an objective genitive, 'faith in Jesus Christ' (as the object of our faith), has come to be questioned; it is suggested that, where faith (*pistis*) is qualified by a genitive, this should be treated as a subjective genitive as in Rom 3.3, 'the faith(fulness) of God'; in the present instance this involves a decision whether the phrase 'for all who believe' simply repeats much the same idea as is involved in the preceding 'through faith in Jesus Christ', although without the mention of the object of faith (Christ) and with the additional qualification, 'all', or whether it in fact introduces a new idea, the human response of faith, a response to the faith(fulness) of Christ, i.e. the faith(fulness) which Christ has and has shown; cf., e.g., Howard, *Paul* esp. 95-6 n. 191 and the lit. cited there; Williams, '"Righteousness"' esp. 274-6. See also the translation offered above for 3.26. It is interesting, however, that Williams holds the *pistis* of Christ to be nearer in sense to the *pistis* of Abraham of Rom 4.12 than to that of God in 3.3: the 'faith(fulness)' of Abraham does not mean his trustworthiness, 'but that he trusted God', trusting God to fulfil the promises made to him. So, 'as the one who distributes the benefits of the *diathēkē*, Christ proved his

trustworthiness by trusting God in complete obedience to the divine will (cf. Rom 5:18-19); if Christ is dependable, it is because he depended absolutely upon God' (ibid. 275). Despite what Williams says, this interpretation seems to me to combine something of the *pistis* /trustworthiness, dependability of God *and* something of the *pistis* /trust, faith of Abraham.

10 On this understanding of this verse and the *kai* there see Cranfield, *Rom* 1, 213.

11 On this rendering cf. Barrett, *Rom* 159.

12 Cf. the reff. cited by Räisänen, 'Verständnis' 93; as one example there is his telling quotation from Dodd, *Rom* 46: 'The whole argument of iii.1-8 is obscure and feeble. ... The argument of the epistle would go much better if this whole section were omitted.'

13 In his '"Hellenists"' 289-93, Räisänen, following a suggestion made by G. Sellin, proposes that we see in the ideas of Rom 2.25-9 and elsewhere in Paul's writings 'Hellenist traditions'; in that he is particularly thinking of Hellenist Christian traditions, although he suggests that these in turn received their impetus and many of their ideas from allegorizing and 'spiritualizing' Jews of the Dispersion (286-8).

14 See the useful summary by M. T. Brauch in E. P. Sanders, *Paul* (1977) 523-542; also recently Hultgren, *Gospel* chap. 2. It is worth noting the considerable grammatical ambiguity of the genitive 'of God': it could be a 'subjective genitive', but only if 'righteousness' is defined as an activity or action of which God is the subject (one sometimes finds the claim that this phrase could be an 'objective genitive', but I find it hard to think of any sense of an action or activity of 'righteousness' such that God could appropriately be described as its object); it could be a 'possessive genitive' in the sense that 'righteousness' is a quality or characteristic that God possesses; it could be a 'genitive of origin or author' in the sense that this is a 'righteousness' that comes from, is given by, God; it could even be what I suppose might be described as a 'genitive of quality' in the sense that it is a 'righteousness' that measures up to God's standards, is valid in the eyes of God, a 'God-sized' righteousness, so to speak. The

important thing to note here is that, if, as argued above, the sense of 'righteousness' may shift from one aspect of its 'field of meaning' to another, then the sense of the genitive may shift with it.

15 See on 'fields of meaning', e.g., Nida, *Science* 50-1, and Nida–Taber, *Theory* 20-2, and also my 'Observations' 86-7.

16 Piper, *Justification* , argues that the sense of 'God's righteousness' in 3.1-8, 25-6 and 9.14-23 is God's 'unswerving commitment always to preserve the honor of his name and display his glory' (203); that glory and God's essential nature are to dispense mercy (and wrath) on whomsoever God chooses (100). That is certainly a central facet of 'God's righteousness' in Romans, but is it all?

17 Cf. the arguments of Hooker, 'Adam', summarized by Barrett, *Adam* 17-19; also my 'Adam' 413-19.

18 This I find far easier than Suhl's suggestion ('Anlaß' 123-4) that 1.20-7 are Paul's accusation of gentiles and that his charges against the Jews start in 1.28; there is little in that verse to mark such a shift of focus.

19 Some have found the universalistic implications of the participle 'being justified' in 3.24, which clearly qualifies the 'all' who have sinned in the previous verse, so uncomfortable that they have resorted to making 22b-23 a parenthesis and have tried to make it qualify instead the 'all who believe' in 22a, despite the fact that this is in a different case (cf. Sanday-Headlam, *Rom* 85-6 and others cited there). However, (1) the grammatical structure of these verses is a good piece of evidence for the thesis that Paul argues from the manner in which God has saved humanity to the nature of the plight from which humanity had to be saved, rather than *vice versa* despite the order of his argument in Romans (see §5 of this chapter); in other words his thesis that all are sinful is based on his conviction that all need to be justified on the basis of God's grace; (2) there is a very real sense in which all are in fact justified in the sense that they are all represented by Christ who was 'raised for our justification' (4.25). Despite all objections to his thesis E. P. Sanders in his *Paul* (1977 and 1983) seems to me at least to have shown that

THE REASONS FOR ROMANS

Paul's representation of his fellow Jews does not do justice to
what Judaism sought to be nor to its own declaration of its
principles, even if that leaves open the possibility that some
Jews misunderstood it as a religion of human achievement (cf.
Räisänen, *Paul* 167-8).

21 Cf. Räisänen, ibid. 51-2.

22 Stowers re-divides the questions and answers here (*Diatribe*
164-5):

Int(erlocutor).

      What then becomes of boasting?

Paul   It is excluded.

Int.   By what sort of law? Of works?

Paul   No, but through the law of faith. For we consider
a man to be justified by faith apart from works of
law. [I would prefer to see the interlocutor's next
question beginning here.] Or is God the God of
Jews only? Is he not the God of Gentiles also?

Int.   Yes, of the Gentiles also. [Or is this the start of
Paul's reply?]

Paul   If he really is (*eiper*), he is the one God [or 'if
indeed there is only one God ...'] who will justify
the circumcised by faith and the uncircumcised
through faith.

Int.   Do we then overthrow the law through faith?

Paul   By no means! On the contrary we uphold the law.

Int.   What then shall we say that Abraham our
forefather according to the flesh found? For if
Abraham was justified by works he has something
to boast about.

Paul   But not before God. For what does the scripture
say? ...

23 Cf. Dodd, *Rom* 64: 'in the sense which "Law" has borne
in most of this discussion it is confusing and misleading to
say that we uphold the Law'.

BIBLIOGRAPHY

ABBREVIATIONS

In general the conventions followed are those of the *Journal of Biblical Literature* 95 (1976) 331–46 (with a preference for the *HTR* forms given there), and G. Kittel, tr. G. W. Bromiley, *Theological Dictionary of the New Testament* 1 (Grand Rapids: Eerdmans, 1964) xvi-xxxix.

In addition note the following:

Comm(s).	Commentary/Commentaries
ET	English translation
ET	*Expository Times*
GCS	Griechische christliche Schriftsteller
JSNT	Journal for the Study of the New Testament
KEK	Kritisch-exegetischer Kommentar über das Neue Testament (Meyers)
Migne *PG*	Migne, J., *Patrologia Graeca*
Migne *PL*	id., *Patrologia Latina*
SCBO	Scriptorum classicorum bibliotheca Oxoniensis
Tr.	Translated/translation

Select Bibliography

A. Primary Sources

Charlesworth, J. H. (ed.), *The Old Testament Pseudepigrapha* (London: Darton, Longman & Todd, 1983-5).

[Demetrius of Phalerum], *On Style* , ed. W. R. Roberts (LCL, London: Heinemann/New York: Putnam, 1927).

Dio Cassius, ed./tr. E. Cary (LCL, London: Heinemann/ New York: Macmillan, 1914-27).

Epiphanius, *Ancoratus, Panarion* , ed. K. Holl (GCS 25, 31, 37, Leipzig: Hinrichs, 1915-33).

Eusebius, *The Ecclesiastical History* (LCL, London: Heinemann/New York: Putnam, 1926-32).

Greek New Testament, The, ed. K. Aland *et al.*, (New York, etc.: United Bible Societies, 1975³).

Hippolytus, *Refutatio omnium haeresium* , ed. P. Wendland (GCS 26, Leipzig: Hinrichs, 1916).

Irenaeus, *Adversus haereses*, ed. W. W. Harvey (Cambridge Univ., 1857).

Josephus, ed./tr. H. St J. Thackeray, R. Marcus *et al.*, (LCL, London: Heinemann/New York: /Cambridge MA: Harvard Univ., 1926-65).

Philo of Alexandria, ed./tr. F. H. Colson, G. H. Whitaker, R. Marcus (LCL, London : Heinemann/New York: Putnam/Cambridge MA: Harvard Univ., 1929-62).

Rießler, *Schrifttum* =Rießler, P. (ed./tr.), *Altjüdisches Schrifttum außerhalb der Bibel* (Heidelberg: Kerle, 1966²).

Sparks, *Apocryphal Old Testament* =Sparks, H. F. D. (ed.), *The Apocryphal Old Testament* (Oxford: Clarendon, 1984).

Suetonius, ed./tr. J. C. Rolfe (LCL, London: Heinemann/ New York: Putnam, 1914).

Tacitus, *Annales*, ed. C. D. Fisher (SCBO, Oxford: Clarendon, 1906).

B. Commentaries on Romans
(Unless otherwise mentioned these are referred to simply by the abbreviation *Rom* or *Röm*)

Achtemeier, P. J., *Romans* (Interpretation, Atlanta: Knox, 1985).

'Ambrosiaster', *Commentaria in epistolam ad Romanos* , in *CSEL* 81.1, ed. H. J. Vogels (1966).

Barrett, C. K., *A Commentary on the Epistle to the Romans* (Black's NT Comm., London: Black, 1962).

Barth, K., *Der Römerbrief* (München: Kaiser, 1929⁶); ET – London: Oxford Univ., 1933;
  id., *A Shorter Commentary on Romans* (London: SCM, 1959) – ET of München: Kaiser, 1956.

Best, E., *The Letter of Paul to the Romans* (Cambridge Bible Comm., Cambridge Univ., 1967).

Black, M., *Romans* (New Century Bible, London: Oliphants, 1973).

Cranfield, *Rom* (ICC)=Cranfield, C. E. B., *A Critical and Exegetical Commentary on the Epistle to the Romans* (ICC, Edinburgh: Clark, 1975-9);
  id., *Romans: a Shorter Commentary* (Edinburgh: Clark, 1985).

Dodd, C. H., *The Epistle of Paul to the Romans* (MNTC, London: Hodder & Stoughton, 1932).

Harrisville, R. A., *Romans* (Augsburg Comm. on the NT, Minneapolis: Augsburg, 1980).

Käsemann, E., *An die Römer* (HNT 8a, Tübingen: Mohr, 1974²); ET – London: SCM, 1980.
Kuss, O., *Der Römerbrief* (Regensburg: Pustet, 1963-).
Leenhardt, F. J., *The Epistle to the Romans* (London: Lutterworth, 1961) – ET of Neuchâtel: Delachaux & Niestlé, 1957.
Lipsius, R. A., *Briefe an die Galater, Römer, Philipper* (HKNT 2.2, Freiburg-i-Br.: Mohr, 1892²).
Michel, O., *Der Brief an die Römer* (KEK, Göttingen: Vandenhoeck & Ruprecht, 1966¹³).
Nygren, A., *Pauli Brev till Romarna* (Tolkning av Nya Testamentet, Stockholm: Svenska Kyrkans Diakonistyretses Bokförlag, 1944); German tr. – Göttingen: Vandenhoeck & Ruprecht, 1965⁴; ET – London: SCM,1952.
O'Neill, J. C., *Paul's Letter to the Romans* (Harmondsworth: Penguin, 1975).
Origen, *Commentaria in epistolam ad Romanos* in Migne, *Patrologia Graeca* 14, 837-1292.
Sanday, W., Headlam, A. C., *A Critical and Exegetical Commentary on the Epistle to the Romans* (ICC, Edinburgh: Clark, 1895, 1902⁵).
Wilckens, U., *Der Brief an die Römer* (EKKNT 6.1-3, Zürich, etc.; Benziger/Neukirchen-Vluyn: Neukirchener, 1978-82).
Zeller, D., *Der Brief an die Römer* (RNT, Regensburg: Pustet, 1985).

C. Secondary Literature

Aland, 'Entstehung'= Aland, K., 'Die Entstehung des Corpus Paulinum', in *Neutestamentliche Entwürfe* (TBü 63, München: Kaiser, 1979) 302-50;
'Schluß'= id., 'Der Schluß und die ursprüngliche Gestalt des Römerbriefes', ibid. 284-301.
Altaner–Stuiber, *Patrologie* =Altaner, B., Stuiber, A., *Patrologie: Leben, Schriften und Lehre der Kirchenväter* (Freiburg-i-Br., etc.: Herder, 1978).

Barrett, *Adam* =Barrett, C. K., *From First Adam to Last: a Study in Pauline Theology* (London: Black, 1962).

Bartsch, 'Situation'=Bartsch, H. W., 'The Historical Situation of Romans', in *Encounter* 33 (1972) 329-38 (ET of *Communio Viatorum* 8 (1965)=*Studia evangelica* 4 (TU 102, Berlin: Akademie, 1968) 281-91).

Baur, 'Zweck'=Baur, F. C., 'Über Zweck und Veranlassung des Römerbriefs und die damit zusammenhängenden Verhältnisse der römischen Gemeinde', in *Tübinger Zeitschrift für Theologie* 3 (1836) 59-178, repr. in *Ausgewählte Werke in Einzelausgaben* 1: *Historisch-kritische Untersuchungen zum Neuen Testament* (Stuttgart/Bad Cannstatt: Frommann, 1963) 147-266.

Beker, *Paul* =Beker, J. C., *Paul the Apostle; the Triumph of God in Life and Thought* (Edinburgh: T. & T. Clark, 1980).

Berger, 'Gattungen'=Berger, K., 'Hellenistische Gattungen im Neuen Testament' in (ed.) H. Temporini, K. Haase, *Aufstieg und Niedergang der römischen Welt* 2.25.2 (Berlin/New York: de Gruyter, 1984) 1031-1432.

Best, E., *Paul and His Converts* (Edinburgh: T. & T. Clark, 1988).

Betz, *Gal* =Betz, H. D., *Galatians: a Commentary on Paul's Letter to the Churches in Galatia* (Hermeneia, Philadelphia: Fortress, 1979).

Bjerkelund, *Parakalô* =Bjerkelund, C. J., *Parakalô: Form, Funktion und Sinn der parakalô-Sätze in den paulinischen Briefen* (Bibliotheca theologica norvegica 1, Oslo, etc.: Universitetsforlaget, 1967).

Borg, 'Context'=Borg, M., 'A New Context for Romans xiii', in *NTS* 19 (1972-3) 205-18.

Bornkamm, G., 'The Letter to the Romans as Paul's Last Will and Testament', in Donfried, *Debate* 17-31 (ET of *Geschichte und Glaube* 2, BEvTh 53, München: Kaiser, 1971, 120-39);
Paul (London: Hodder & Stoughton, 1971) – ET of Stuttgart: Kohlhammer, 1969.

Borse, "Einordnung'=Borse, U., "Die geschichtliche und theologische Einordnung des Römerbriefes', in *BZ* 16 (1972) 70-83.

Brauch, M. T., 'Perspectives on "God's Righteousness" in Recent German Discussion', in E. P. Sanders, *Paul and Palestinian Judaism: a Comparison of Patterns of Religion* (London: SCM, 1977) 523-42.

Brown–Meier, *Antioch* =Brown, R. E., Meier, J. P., *Antioch and Rome: New Testament Cradles of Catholic Christianity* (London: Chapman, 1983).

Bruce, F. F., 'The Epistles of Paul' in (ed.) H. H. Rowley, M. Black, *Peake's Commentary on the Bible* (London, etc.: Nelson, 1962) 927-39;
Gal =id., *The Epistle to the Galatians: a Commentary on the Greek Text* (Exeter: Paternoster, 1982);
Paul =id., *Paul: Apostle of the Free Spirit* (Exeter: Paternoster, 1977).

Campbell, 'Debate'=Campbell, W. S., 'The Romans Debate' in *JSNT* 10 (1981) 19-28;
'Paul'=id., 'Why Did Paul Write Romans?' in *ET* 85 (1974) 264-9;
'Romans III'=id., 'Romans III as a Key to the Structure and Thought of the Letter' in *NovT* 23 (1981) 22-40.

Dahl, 'Theology'=Dahl, N. A., 'The Missionary Theology in the Epistle to the Romans', in *Studies in Paul: Theology for the Early Christian Mission* (Minneapolis: Augsburg, 1977) 70-94.

Donfried, *Debate* =Donfried, K. P. (ed.), *The Romans Debate* (Minneapolis: Augsburg, 1977);
id., 'False Presuppositions in the Study of Romans', in *Debate* 120-48 (repr. from *CBQ* 36, 1974, 332-55).

Drane, 'Paul'=Drane, J. W., 'Why Did Paul Write Romans?' in (ed.) D. A. Hagner, M. J. Harris, *Pauline Studies: Essays Presented to Professor F. F. Bruce on His 70th Birthday* (Exeter: Paternoster/Grand Rapids MI: Eerdmans, 1980) 208-27.

Dunn, *Unity* =Dunn, J.D.G., *Unity and Diversity in the New Testament: an Inquiry into the Character of Earliest Christianity* (London: SCM, 1977).

Enslin, M., *Reapproaching Paul* (Philadelphia: Westminster, 1972).

Fiorenza, 'Situation'=Fiorenza, E. S., 'Rhetorical Situation and Historical Reconstruction in 1 Corinthians', in *NTS* 33 (1987) 386-403.

Friedrich-Pöhlmann-Stuhlmacher, 'Situation'=Friedrich, J., Pöhlmann, W., Stuhlmacher, P., 'Zur historischen Situation und Intention von Römer 13, 1-7', in *ZThK* 73 (1976) 131-66.

Fuchs, *Hermeneutik* =Fuchs, E., *Hermeneutik* (Bad Cannstatt: Müllerschön, 1963³).

Furnish, *Love Command* =Furnish, V. P., *The Love Command in the New Testament* (London: SCM, 1973).

Gamble, *History* =Gamble, H., *The Textual History of the Letter to the Romans* (Studies and Documents 42, Grand Rapids MI: Eerdmans, 1977).

Georgi, *Geschichte* =Georgi, D., *Die Geschichte der Kollekte des Paulus für Jerusalem* (ThF 38, Hamburg-Bergstedt: Reich, 1965).

Grundmann, W., 'The Christ-Statements of the New Testament', in *TDNT* 6 (1974) 537-73.

Gunther, *Opponents* =Gunther, J. J., *St Paul's Opponents and Their Background: a Study of Apocalyptic and Jewish Sectarian Teachings* (NovTSup 35, Leiden: Brill, 1973).

Haenchen, *Apostelgeschichte* =Haenchen, E., *Die Apostelgeschichte* (KEK 3, Göttingen: Vandenhoeck & Ruprecht, 1977¹⁶).

Harder, 'Anlaß' =Harder, G., 'Der konkrete Anlaß des Römerbriefes', in *Theologia Viatorum* 6 (1954) 13-24.

Herold, *Zorn* =Herold, G., *Zorn und Gerechtigkeit Gottes bei Paulus; eine Unterschung zu Röm. 1,16–18*, Europäische Hochschulschriften Reihe 23 (Theologie) 14, Bern/Frankfurt: Lang, 1973.

Hock, *Context* =Hock, R. F., *The Social Context of Paul's Ministry: Tentmaking and Apostleship* (New Haven/ London: Yale Univ., 1983).

Hooker, 'Adam'=Hooker, M. D., 'Adam in Romans i', in *NTS* 6 (1959-60) 297-306.

Howard, *Paul* =Howard, G., *Paul: Crisis in Galatia: a Study in Early Christian Theology* (SNTSMS 35, Cambridge Univ., 1979).

Hultgren, *Gospel* =Hultgren, A., *Paul's Gospel and Mission: the Outlook from His Letter to the Romans* (Philadelphia: Fortress, 1985).

Jeremias, *Words* =Jeremias, J., *The Eucharistic Words of Jesus* (London: SCM, 1966; ET of Göttingen: Vandenhoeck & Ruprecht, 1960³, with revisions).

Jervell, J., 'The Letter to Jerusalem', in Donfried, *Debate* 61-74.

Jewett, 'Agitators'=Jewett, R., 'The Agitators and the Galatian Congregation', in *NTS* 17 (1970-1) 198-212; *Dating* =id., *Dating Paul's Life* (London: SCM, 1979); 'Romans'=id., 'Romans as an Ambassadorial Letter', in *Interpretation* 36 (1982) 5-20.

Karris, R. J., 'Romans 14:1-15:13 and the Occasion of Romans', in Donfried, *Debate* 75-99 (repr. of *CBQ* 35, 1973, 155-78).

Kaye, B. N., '"To the Romans and Others" Revisited', in *NovT* 18 (1976) 37-77.

Keck, *Paul* =Keck, L. E., *Paul and His Letters* (Proclamation Commentaries, Philadelphia: Fortress, 1979).

Kettunen, *Abfassungszweck* =Kettunen, M., *Der Abfassungszweck des Römerbriefes* (Annales Academiae scientarum Fennicae: dissertationes humanarum litterarum 18, Helsinki: Suomalainen Tiedeakatemia, 1979).

Klein, 'Purpose'=Klein, G., 'Paul's Purpose in Writing the Epistle to the Romans', in Donfried, *Debate* 32-49 (ET of *Rekonstruktion und Interpretation: Gesammelte*

Aufsätze zum Neuen Testament , BEvTh 50, München: Kaiser, 1969, 129-44).

Klijn–Reinink, *Evidence* =Klijn, A. F. J., Reinink, G. J., *Patristic Evidence for Jewish Christian Sects* (NovTSup 36, Leiden: Brill, 1973).

Knox, *Chapters* =Knox, J., *Chapters in a Life of Paul* (London: Black, 1954).

Kümmel, *Introduction* ²=Kümmel, W. G., *Introduction to the New Testament* (London: SCM, 1975²); 'Probleme'=id., 'Die Probleme von Römer 9-11 in der gegenwärtigen Forschungslage' in (ed.) L. de Lorenzi, *Die Israelfrage nach Römer 9-11* (Monographische Reihe von "Benedictina": biblisch-ökumenische Abteilung 3, Rom: Abtei von St Paul vor den Mauern, 1977) 13-33.

Lightfoot, J. B., *Saint Paul's Epistle to the Philippians* (London: Macmillan, 1885⁸).

Lüdemann, *Christentum* = Lüdemann, G., *Das frühe Christentum nach der Tradition der Apostelgeschichte: ein Kommentar* (Göttingen: Vandenhoeck & Ruprecht, 1987); *Paulus* 1=id., *Paulus der Heidenapostel* 1: *Studien zur Chronologie* (FRLANT 123, Göttingen: Vandenhoeck & Ruprecht, 1980); ET – Philadelphia: Fortress, 1984.

Luz, 'Aufbau'=Luz, U., 'Zum Aufbau von Röm. 1-8' in *ThZ* 25 (1969) 161-81.

Manson, T. W., 'St Paul's Letter to the Romans – and Others', in Donfried, *Debate* 1-16.

Melanchthon, P., *Loci communes* of 1521, in *Melanchthons Werke im Auswahl* 2.1, ed. H. Engelland (Gütersloh: Bertelsmann, 1952) 1-163.

Metzger, *Commentary* =Metzger, B. M., *A Textual Commentary on the Greek New Testament* (London/ New York: United Bible Societies, 1971).

Moxnes, *Theology* = Moxnes, H., *Theology in Conflict: Studies in Paul's Understanding of God in Romans* (NovTSup 53, Leiden: Brill, 1980).

Nickle, *Collection* =Nickle, K. F., *The Collection: a Study in the Strategy of Paul* (SBT 48, London: SCM, 1966).

Nida, *Science* =Nida, E. A., *Toward a Science of Translating with Special Reference to Principles and Procedures Involved in Bible Translating* (Leiden: Brill, 1964).

Nida-Taber, *Theory* = Nida, E. A., Taber, C. R., *The Theory and Practice of Translation* (Helps for Translators 8, Leiden: Brill, 1974).

Ollrog, W. H., 'Die Abfassungsverhältnisse von Röm 16', in (ed.) D. Lührmann, G. Strecker, *Kirche: Festschrift für Günther Bornkamm zum 75. Geburtstag* (Tübingen: Mohr, 1980) 221-44.

Osten-Sacken, P. von der, *Römer 8* = *Römer 8 als Beispiel paulinischer Soteriologie* (FRLANT 112, Göttingen: Vandenhoeck & Ruprecht, 1975).

Piper, 'Demonstration'=Piper, J., 'The Demonstration of the Righteousness of God in Romans 3:25, 26', in *JSNT* 7 (1980) 2-32;
Justification = id., *The Justification of God: an Exegetical and Theological Study of Romans 9:1-23* (Grand Rapids: Baker, 1983).

Räisänen, '"Hellenists"' =Räisänen, H., 'The "Hellenists" – a Bridge between Jesus and Paul?', in id., *Torah = The Torah and Christ: Essays in German and English on the Problem of the Law in Early Christianity* (Publications of the Finnish Exegetical Society 45, Helsinki, 1986) 242-306;
Paul = id., *Paul and the Law* (WUNT 29, Tübingen: Mohr, 1983);
'Verständnis' = id., 'Zum Verständnis von Röm 3,1-8', in *Studien zum Neuen Testament und seiner Umwelt* 10 (1985) 93-108; repr. in id., *Torah* 185-205.

Sanders, *Paul* (1977)=Sanders, E. P., *Paul and Palestinian Judaism: a Comparison of Patterns of Religion* (London: SCM, 1977);

Paul (1983)=id., *Paul, the Law and the Jewish People* (Philadelphia: Fortress, 1983).

Schmeller, *Paulus* =Schmeller, T., *Paulus und die 'Diatribe': eine vergleichende Stilinterpretation* (NTAbh Neue Folge 19, Münster: Aschendorff, 1987).

Schmithals, *Römerbrief* =Schmithals, W., *Der Römerbrief als historisches Problem* (StNT 9, Gütersloh: Mohn, 1975).

Schrenk, 'Römerbrief'=Schrenk, G., 'Der Römerbrief als Missionsdokument', in id., *Studien zu Paulus* (AThANT 26, Zürich: Zwingli, 1954) 81-106.

Schürer, *History* =Schürer, E., *The History of the Jewish People in the Age of Jesus Christ (175 B.C. - A.D. 135)*, ed. G. and P. Vermes, F. Millar, M. Black (Edinburgh: Clark, 1973-87).

Stirewalt, M. L., 'The Form and Function of the Greek Letter-Essay', in Donfried, *Debate* 175-206.

Stowers, *Diatribe* =Stowers, S. K., *The Diatribe and Paul's Letter to the Romans* (SBL Diss. Series 57, Chico: Scholars, 1981);
Letter Writing =id., *Letter Writing in Greco-Roman Antiquity* (Philadelphia: Westminster, 1986).

Suggs, '"Word"'=Suggs, M. J., '"The word is near you": Romans 10:6-10 within the Purpose of the Letter' in (ed.) W. R. Farmer, C. F. D. Moule, *Christian History and Interpretation: Studies Presented to John Knox* (Cambridge Univ., 1967) 289-312.

Suhl, 'Anlaß' = Suhl, A., 'Der konkrete Anlaß des Römerbriefes', in *Kairos* 13 (1971) 119-30;
Paulus = id., *Paulus und seine Briefe: ein Beitrag zur paulinischen Chronologie* (StNT 11, Gütersloh: Mohn, 1975).

Theißen, *Setting* =Theißen, G., *The Social Setting of Pauline Christianity* (Studies of the NT and Its World, Edinburgh: Clark, 1982).

Watson, *Paul* =Watson, F., *Paul, Judaism and the Gentiles: a Sociological Approach* (SNTSMS 56, Cambridge Univ., 1986).

Wedderburn, 'Adam'= Wedderburn, A. J. M., 'Adam in Paul's Letter to the Romans', in *Studia Biblica* 3: *Papers on Paul and Other New Testament Writers* , ed. E. A. Livingstone (JSNTS Supplements Series 3, Sheffield: JSOT, 1980) 413-30;
'Chronologies'=id., 'Some Recent Pauline Chronologies', in *ET* 92 (1981) 103-8;
'Observations'=id., 'Some Observations on Paul's Use of the Phrases "in Christ" and "with Christ" ', in *JSNT* 25 (1985) 83-97;
'Purpose'=id., 'The Purpose and Occasion of Romans Again', in *ET* 90 (1979) 137-41.

White, *Light* =White, J. L., *Light from Ancient Letters* (Philadelphia: Fortress, 1986).

Wiefel, W., 'The Jewish Community in Ancient Rome and the Origins of Roman Christianity', in Donfried, *Debate* 100-19.

Wilckens, 'Abfassungszweck' =Wilckens, U., 'Über Abfassungszweck und Aufbau des Römerbriefes', in id., *Rechtfertigung als Freiheit: Paulusstudien* (Neukirchen: Neukirchener, 1974) 110-70.

Williams, '"Righteousness"' =Williams, S. K., 'The "Righteousness of God" in Romans', in *JBL* 99 (1980) 241-90.

Zeller, *Juden* =Zeller, D., *Juden und Heiden in der Mission des Paulus: Studien zum Römerbrief* (Forschung zur Bibel 8, Stuttgart: Katholisches Bibelwerk, 1976).

INDEX OF NEW TESTAMENT PASSAGES
CITED

THE REASONS FOR ROMANS

Romans — *cont.*		Romans — *cont.*		Romans — *cont.*	
3.3	112, 150	4.25	110, 121, 130, 152	7.6	135
3.4	112, 118	5	132, 135	7.7	131, 133
3.4-5	109, 112	5-8	130-6, 138	7.7ff	131
3.5	116	5.1	110, 130-1	7.7-13	136
3.7	112	5.1-2	132	7.7-25	133-5, 138
3.7-8	114	5.1-11	106, 130-2	7.12	111, 133
3.8	2, 114-15, 126, 134	5.1-21	130	7.13	131
3.9	119	5.2-3	106-7	7.13-25	133
3.10	109	5.2-5	106	7.25	131
3.10-18	127	5.3-4	131	8	106, 131-2, 135
3.20	119, 125-6	5.3-5	86	8.1ff	131
3.20-2	109	5.5	84, 106, 135	8.3	95
3.20-4.25	138	5.6	95	8.4	84, 111, 135
3.21	105, 116, 127-9	5.6-10	132	8.7-8	132
3.21ff	131	5.7	110, 131	8.10	111, 116
3.22-3	119, 125, 131, 152	5.8	95	8.11, 15	95
3.23	36, 138	5.9	110, 132	8.17	131, 135
3.24	109, 120, 152	5.9-11	131-2	8.18ff	131
3.24-5	121	5.11	107, 132	8.20-1	106, 133
3.24-6	95	5.12-21	131-2	8.24-5	105-6, 135
3.25	116	5.12-11.36	25	8.26	132
3.25-6	109-10, 117, 152	5.15	132	8.29-30	95
3.26	150-1	5.16-19	110	8.30	111
3.27	107, 128	5.17	116, 132	8.31-9	132
3.27ff	153	5.18-19	151	8.32	95
3.28	110	5.20	114, 132-3	8.33	111
3.28-30	128	5.20-1	131, 133	8.34	95, 108
3.30	110	5.21	110, 116	8.37	95
3.31	128, 134	6-8	130, 135	8.38	135
3.31-4.25	138	6.1	114, 131, 133-4	8.38-9	107
4	36, 116, 118, 129	6.1ff	131	9-11	4, 7, 87-91,
4.2	107, 110	6.1-7.25	133-4, 136, 138		112-13, 127, 130,
4.3	36, 110	6.4	95		136-8, 148
4.3-9	120	6.7	110	9.1	130, 136
4.5-6	110	6.9	95	9.1-5	113
4.7-8	121	6.13	110	9.4-5	90
4.9, 11	110	6.14	35, 131, 133	9.14	111, 113
4.12	150	6.15-7.6	114, 131,	9.14-23	152
4.13	110		133-4, 137	9.15	75
4.17	95, 121	6.16, 18-20	110-11	9.15-17	88
4.18	105-6	6.21; 7.1-6	134	9.15-18	81
4.19	129	7.4	95	9.17-18	113
4.22	110	7.5	134-5	9.18	88
4.24-5	95	7.5-6	131, 133	9.20-2	117

INDEX OF NEW TESTAMENT PASSAGES CITED